Reprint Publishing

FOR PEOPLE WHO GO FOR ORIGINALS.

www.reprintpublishing.com

A LIST OF

AMERICAN DRAMAS

IN THE NEW YORK PUBLIC LIBRARY

NEW YORK
PUBLIC LIBRARY
1916

NOTE

A few plays by English authors have been included in this list. In all cases these are plays written by authors whose long residence here has identified them with America. A few adaptations of plays originally written by European authors have also been included under the names of the adapters.

To the list as it first appeared in the Bulletin a number of titles have been added, while a few errors have been corrected. A title index has also been added. Thanks are due to Professor Brander Matthews, of Columbia University, and, President F. W. Atkinson, of the Polytechnic Institute of Brooklyn, for suggestions and criticism.

The plays in this list are in the Reference Department of the Library, and must be consulted in the Central Building, Fifth Avenue and Forty-second Street. They may not be borrowed for use outside the building.

The Branches of the Library own many standard and many contemporary plays which may be borrowed for home use.

REPRINTED JANUARY 1916
FROM THE
BULLETIN OF THE NEW YORK PUBLIC LIBRARY
OF OCTOBER 1915

form p-59 [xi-3-15 250]

LIST OF AMERICAN DRAMAS IN THE
NEW YORK PUBLIC LIBRARY

COMPILED BY DANIEL C. HASKELL

Adams, Justin. The limit of the law. A drama in five acts. Boston: W. H. Baker ₁cop. 1896₁. 40 p. 12°. (Baker's edition of plays.) **NBL p.v.5, no.15**

Adams, Oscar Fay. A motley jest: Shakespearean diversions. ₁A Shakespearean fantasy. The merchant of Venice: act sixth.₁ Boston: Sherman, French & Co., 1909. 5 p.l., 64 p. 12°. ***NCS**

Aiken, George L. Uncle Tom's cabin; or, Life among the lowly. A domestic drama, in six acts. Dramatized by George L. Aiken. New York: S. French ₁1858?₁. 60 p. 12°. (French's standard drama. no. 217.) **NCOF**
The Library has three prompter's copies, each interleaved, and with ms. notes.

Akins, Zoë. Papa; an amorality in three acts. New York: Mitchell Kennerley, 1913. ix, 95 p. 12°. (Modern drama series.) **NBM**

Aladdin; or, The wonderful lamp. A drama in three acts. As produced at Barnum's Museum, New York, March 17th, 1856... New York: O. A. Roorbach, Jr., 1856. 2 p.l., (1)4–22 p. 12°. (The acting drama. no. 18.) **NBM p.v.4**

Alderman, Joseph Sorell. The net. (Yale Sheffield monthly. New Haven, 1915. 8°. v. 22, p. 5–14.) **OA**

Aldrich, Thomas Bailey. Mercedes, and later lyrics. Boston: Houghton, Mifflin and Company, 1884. 111 p. 12°. **NBI**

—— Pauline Pavlova. A drama in one act. ₁In verse.₁ Boston: Houghton, Mifflin & Co. ₁cop. 1890.₁ 1 p.l., 11 p. 12°. **NBL p.v.6, no.2**

—— The set of turquoise: a dramatic sketch. (In his: The ballad of Babie Bell, and other poems. New York, 1859. 12°. p. 85–112.) **NBI**

Alexander, William Patterson. Queen Kapiolani. (Yale Sheffield monthly. New Haven, 1914. 8°. v. 21, p. 117–123.) **OA**

Allen, Ethan. Washington; or, The Revolution. A drama...founded upon the historic events of the war for American independence... London: F. T. Neely ₁cop. 1894–99₁. 2 v. in 1. 12°. **NBM**

Allender, George. Imbroglio: a drama. San Francisco: S. Carson & Co., 1885. 186 p. 12°. **NBM**

Allingham, John Till. 'Tis all a farce. A farce, in two acts. ₁By J. T. Allingham.₁ As performed at the Philadelphia Theatre. Philadelphia: published by R. H. Lanfestey, 1834. 30 p. 16°. (Lanfestey's edition.) **NBL p.v.16, no.1**

An **American** wife. A comedy in four acts. ₁18—?₁ 4 pamphlets. 4°. **†NCOF**
Prompter's copy, typewritten.

Amory, Esmerie. The epistolary flirt, in four exposures. Chicago: Way & Williams, 1896. 100 p., 1 l. 16°. **NBM**

Anderson, Edward Lowell. Nero, the parricide; an historical play in four acts. ₁By E. L. Anderson.₁ ₁In verse.₁ ₁Cincinnati,₁ 1870. 47 p. 8°. **NBL p.v.11, no.12**

Andre, R. Food for powder. A vaudeville ₁in 2 acts₁. Chicago: The Dramatic Pub. Co. ₁1891.₁ 24 p. 12°. (American amateur drama.) **NBL p.v.5, no.7**

The **Animated** portrait. An extravaganza in three acts. n. p., n. d. 33 p. 12°. **NBL p.v.21, no.1**

Armstrong, L. O. Hiawatha or Nanabozho. An Ojibway Indian play. Descriptive notes and excerpts ₁from Longfellow's Hiawatha₁ to be used as a libretto for Hiawatha or Nanabozho, an Ojibway Indian play. n. p., 1901. 30 p. illus. 8°. **NBL p.v.25, no.1**

Arnold, Alexander Streeter. In the nick of time. A serio-comic drama in three acts. Boston: W. H. Baker & Co. ₁cop. 1892.₁ 35 p. 12°. (Baker's edition of plays.) **NBL p.v.19, no.19**

Arnold, George, and FRANK CAHILL. Parlor theatricals: or, Winter evenings' entertainment... New York: Dick & Fitzgerald ₁cop. 1859₁. 3 p.l., 9–152 p. 12°. **MZB**

Arnold, James Oliver. Historical drama and tableaux, Uncle Tom's freedom... ₁Dayton, O.,₁ 1893. 36 p. 8°. **NBL p.v.25, no.2**

Arnold, Samuel James. The devil's bridge. an opera, in three acts. Philadelphia: T. H. Palmer, 1822. 55 p. 16°. **NCOF**

Prompter's copy, interleaved. With ms. notes.

Around the world in eighty days. A dramatization of Jules Verne's story, in twelve tableaux. [18—?] 2 p.l., 148 l. f°. † **NCOF**

Prompter's copy, in manuscript.

Austin, J. J. The golden age to come: or, The victory of faith, and hope, and love. A sacred drama, written for the people. Boston: A. Tompkins, 1854. 124 p. 12°. **NBM**

Austin, Martha Waddill. Tristram and Isoult. [A drama.] Boston: The Poet Lore Co., 1905. 64 p. 12°. **NBI**

Austin, Mary. The arrow maker; a drama in three acts. New York: Duffield and Company, 1911. xiii, 128 p., 1 port. 12°. **NBM**

Bacon, Delia. The bride of Fort Edward, founded on an incident of the Revolution. [By Delia Bacon.] New York: S. Colman, 1839. viii, 9–174 p. 12°. **NBM**

Bacon, Josephine Dodge Daskam. The twilight of the gods. (Forum. New York, 1915. 8°. v. 53, p. 7–20.) ***DA**

Bagg, Helen F. His model wife: a comedy in one act. Philadelphia: The Penn Publishing Co., 1908. 28 p. 12°. **NBL p.v.6, no.13**

—— Untangling Tony: a comedy in two acts. Philadelphia: The Penn Publishing Co., 1908. 38 p. 12°. **NBL p.v.6, no.1**

Bailey, John J. Waldimar. A tragedy, in five acts. New York: [James Van Norden, prtr.,] 1834. 124 p., 1 l., 6 p. 8°. **NBM**

Baily, William Entriken. Dramatic poems. Philadelphia: the author, 1894. 117 p. 16°. **NBM**

The sacrifice of Iphigenia. Priam, king of Troy. Andromache in captivity. The daughters of Œdipus.

Baker, George Melville. Above the clouds. Boston: W. H. Baker & Co. [cop. 1889.] 1 p.l., 99–168 p. 12°. (Baker's edition of plays.) **NBM (Baker), p.v.1**

—— Among the breakers. A drama in two acts. Boston: W. H. Baker & Co. [cop. 1889.] 1 p.l., 107–170 p., 1 pl. 12°. (Baker's edition of plays.) **NBM (Baker), p.v.1**

—— Better than gold. A drama in four acts. Boston: W. H. Baker & Co. [cop. 1889.] 58 p., 1 pl. 12°. (Baker's edition of plays.) **NBM (Baker), p.v.1**

—— Bread on the waters. A drama in two acts. Boston: W. H. Baker & Co. [cop. 1889.] 1 p.l., 221–290 p. 12°. (Baker's edition of plays.) **NBM (Baker), p.v.1**

—— The champion of her sex. (For female characters only.) Boston: W. H.

Baker & Co. [cop. 1874.] 1 p.l., 109–131 p. 12°. (The amateur drama.) **NAFH p.v.1, no.7**

—— Comrades. A drama in three acts. Boston: W. H. Baker & Co. [cop. 1889.] 52 p. 12°. (Baker's edition of plays.) **NBM (Baker), p.v.1**

—— Down by the sea. A drama. Boston: W. H. Baker & Co. [cop. 1889.] 1 p.l., 7–61 p. 12°. (Baker's edition of plays.) **NBM (Baker), p.v.1**

—— The drawing-room stage: a series of original dramas, comedies, farces, and entertainments for amateur theatricals and school exhibitions. Boston: Lee & Shepard, 1873. 274 p., 3 pl. illus. 12°. **MZB**

My brother's keeper. The revolt of the bees. A tender attachment. Among the breakers. Gentlemen of the jury. The seven ages. The Boston dip. The duchess of Dublin.

—— Enlisted for the war. A drama. Boston: Geo. M. Baker & Co. [cop. 1874.] 1 p.l., 9–81 p. 12°. (Spencer's universal stage.) **NBL p.v.5, no.16**

—— Gentlemen of the jury. A farce [in one act]. Boston: G. M. Baker & Co. [cop. 1873.] 1 p.l., 171–186 p. 12°. (The amateur drama.) **NBL p.v.5, no.8**

—— The last loaf. A drama. Boston: W. H. Baker & Co. [cop. 1898.] 1 p.l., 7–56 p. 12°. (Baker's edition of plays.) **NBM (Baker), p.v.1**

—— Little brown jug. Boston: W. H. Baker & Co. [cop. 1876.] 1 p.l., 269–332 p. 12°. (Baker's edition of plays.) **NBM (Baker), p.v.1**

—— Nevada; or, The lost mine. A drama in three acts. Boston: W. H. Baker & Co. [cop. 1882.] 55 p. 12°. (Baker's edition of plays.) **NBM (Baker), p.v.1**

—— Our folks. A play in three acts. Dramatized from: Running to waste...by the same author. Boston: W. H. Baker & Co. [cop. 1879.] 78 p. 12°. (Baker's edition of plays.) **NBM (Baker), p.v.1**

—— Sylvia's soldier. A comedy in two acts. Boston: W. H. Baker & Co. [cop. 1893.] 5–48 p. 12°. (The amateur drama.) **NBL p.v.18, no.17**

—— The tempter; or, The sailor's return. Boston: W. H. Baker & Co. [cop. 1894.] 1 p.l., 74–92 p. 12°. (Baker's edition of plays.) **NBM (Baker), p.v.1**

Baker, Rachel E. Her picture. A comedy in one act. Boston: W. H. Baker & Co. [cop. 1894.] 17 p. 12°. (Baker's novelties.) **NBL p.v.19, no.4**

—— Mr. Bob. A comedy in two acts ... Boston: W. H. Baker & Co. [cop. 1894.] 34 p. 12°. (Baker's edition of plays.) **NBL p.v.9, no.10**

Bamburgh, William Cushing. Giacomo: a Venetian tale. New York: privately printed for the author, 1892. 19 l. 8°. **NBL p.v.26, no.4**

Bangs, John Kendrick. The bicyclers. New York: Harper & Bros. [cop. 1896.] 3 p.l., 40 p. 16°. **NBL p.v.31, no.7**

—— A chafing-dish party. New York: Harper & Bros. [cop. 1896.] 2 p.l., (1)4-46 p. 16°. **NBL p.v.31, no.5**

—— A dramatic evening. New York: Harper & Bros. [cop. 1896.] 3 p.l., 44 p. 16°. **NBL p.v.31, no.10**

—— The fatal message. New York: Harper & Bros. [cop. 1896.] 2 p.l., 41 p. 16°. **NBL p.v.31, no.9**

—— Katharine: a travesty. [In four acts.] [New York: Gilliss Brothers & Turnure,] 1888. 2 p.l., (1)4-127(1) p. 16°. **NBX**

—— Mephistopheles: a profanation. New York: Gilliss Bros. & Turnure, 1889. 97 p. 16°. **NBX**

—— A proposal under difficulties. A farce. New York: Harper & Bros., 1905. 2 p.l., 70 p., 1 pl. 24°. **NBM**

—— The real thing, and three other farces. New York: Harper & Bros., 1909. 4 p.l., 135 p., 4 pl. 12°. **NBM**
The real thing. The Barringtons' "at home." The return of Christmas. The side-show.

—— The tables turned. A farce in one act. (In: Harper's book of little plays [for children]. New York, 1910. 12°. p. 91-110.] **NBL**

—— The worsted man. A musical play for amateurs. New York: Harper & Bros., 1905. vii, 86 p., 6 pl. 24°. **NBX**

—— The young folk's minstrels. New York: Harper & Bros. [cop. 1897.] 2 p.l., (1)4-26 p. 16°. **NBL p.v.31, no.8**

Banks, Charles Eugene. An American woman, a drama in four acts. Chicago: The Dramatic Pub. Co., cop. 1905. 51 p. 12°. (Sergel's acting drama. no. 77.) **NBL p.v.4, no.3**

Banning, Kendall. "Copy." A one-act newspaper play... Chicago: Clinic Publishing Company, 1910. 28 p., 1 l. 8°. **NBM**

Bannister, Nathaniel H. Putnam, the iron son of '76. A national military drama in three acts... Boston: W. V. Spencer [1859]. 30 p. 12°. **NBM p.v.4**

Barbee, Lindsey. After the game. A college comedy in two acts. Chicago: T. S. Denison [1907]. 31 p. 12°. (Denison's acting plays.) **NBL p.v.5, no.3**

Barbour, Ralph Henry. The conspirators; a Christmas play. (New England magazine. Boston. 1907. 8°. v. 37, p. 425-432.) ***DA**

Barker, Benjamin Fordyce. The rise in Harlem. A comedy. In five acts. [By B. F. Barker.] New York: [privately printed by Baker & Godwin,] 1864. 67 p. 12°. **NBM**

Barker, James Nelson. How to try a lover. A comedy in three acts. [By J. N. Barker.] New York: D. Longworth, 1817. 67 p. 16°. **NBM p.v.10**

—— The Indian princess; or, La belle sauvage. An operatic melo-drame, in three acts... Philadelphia: printed by T. & G. Palmer for G. E. Blake, 1808. iv p., 1 l., 7-74 p. 16°. **NBM p.v.10**
Based on the story of Captain Smith and Pocahontas.

—— Marmion; or, The battle of Flodden Field. A drama in five acts. New York: D. Longworth, 1816. vii(i), 9-79(1) p. 16°. **NBM p.v.10**

—— Tears and smiles: a comedy, in five acts. New York: D. Longworth, 1808. iv p., 1 l., 7-85 p. 16°. **NBM p.v.10**

Barnes, Charlotte M. S. Plays, prose, and poetry. Philadelphia: E. H. Butler & Co., 1848. viii p., 4 l., 13-489 p., 1 l. 8°. **NBY**

The plays included in this volume are Octavia Bragaldi; or, The Confession, and The forest princess; or, Two centuries ago.

Barney the baron. A farce in one act. New York: S. French [18—?]. 16 p. 12°. **NCOF**

Prompter's copy, interleaved. With ms. notes.

Barrie Americanus Neutralis, pseud. The night. English diplomacy and the Triple Entente. A phantasmagoria in one act. (Open court. Chicago, 1915. 8°. v. 29, p. 137-150.) ***DA**

Barrymore, William. Wallace: the hero of Scotland. An historical drama... Boston: W. V. Spencer [18—?]. 30 p. nar. 12°. (Spencer's Boston theatre. no. 48.) **NCOF**

Prompter's copy, interleaved. With mss. notes.

Bartlett, Archie E. Dramas of camp and cloister. Boston: Richard G. Badger [cop. 1907]. 2 p.l., 252 p. 12°. **NBM**
Rahna's triumph. The last judgment. Five acts of love. Love's enchantment. Empire of Talinis.

Barton, Andrew, pseud. See **Forrest,** Thomas.

Bassett, Willard. A gold brick. A farce in one act. Chicago: The Dramatic Publishing Company [cop. 1903]. 8 p. 12°. (The darkey & comic drama.) **NBL p.v.11, no.7**

Batchelder, Clara Burbank. Anne, of old Salem. A drama in three acts. Chicago: The Dramatic Pub. Co., cop. 1906. 41 p. 12°. (Sergel's acting drama. no. 580.) **NBL p.v.4, no.12**

—— Billy's chorus girl. A comedietta... Chicago: T. S. Denison [1907]. 16 p. 12°. (Amateur series.) **NBL p.v.6, no.14**

Bateman, Mrs. Sidney F. Self: an original comedy, in three acts. New York: S. French [1856]. 46 p. 12°. (French's standard drama. no. 163.) **NBM p.v.2**

Bates, Ella Skinner. The convention of the Muses. A classical play for parlor and school. Boston: W. H. Baker & Co., 1902. 8 p. 12°. (Baker's edition of plays.)
NBL p.v.18, no.19

Bates, Esther W. Engaging Janet: a farce in one act. Philadelphia: The Penn Publishing Co., 1908. 18 p. 12°.
NBL p.v.6, no.8

Bates, William Oscar. Jacob Leisler; a play of old New York, with an introductory note by Mrs. Schuyler Van Rensselaer. New York: M. Kennerley, 1913. 1 p.l., xi, 248 p., 1 port. 12°.   NBM

The Battle of Brooklyn, a farce of two acts: as it was performed at Long-Island, On Tuesday the 27th of August, 1776. By the Representatives of the Tyrants of America, Assembled at Philadelphia. Edinburgh: Printed in the Year M,DCC,LXXVII. 35 p. 12°.   Reserve

—— New York, printed for J. Rivington, in the year of the rebellion, 1776. Reprinted: Brooklyn, 1873. 45 p. 8°. (Long Island publications. no. 1.) NBL p.v.10, no.9

Bausman, W. Early California; a drama, in five acts. San Francisco. 1872. 42 p., 1 l. 16°.   NBL p.v.14, no.3

Beach, L. Jonathan Postfree; or, The honest Yankee. A musical farce in three acts. New York: D. Longworth, 1807. 38 p. 16°.   NBM p.v.9

Beale, William Thomas. The chancellor of Egypt. A dramatization of the Bible story of Joseph and his brethren in four acts. Boston: the author, 1905. 1 p.l., 56 p. 8°.   NBL p.v.11, no.11

Beede, Aaron McGaffey. Sitting Bull — Custer. [A drama in four scenes and in verse.] Bismarck, N. D.: Bismarck Tribune Co. [1913.] 7 p.l., 50 p., 2 pl. illus. 8°.   HBC

Beete, comedian. The man of the times: or, A scarcity of cash. A farce. As performed, with universal applause, at the Church-street theatre, Charleston. Written by Mr. Beete, comedian. Charleston: Printed by W. P. Young [1797]. 2 p.l., 38 p. 12°.   Reserve

Bell, Archie. Seralmo. New York: F. T. Neely [cop. 1901]. 2 p.l., 91 p. 12°.
NBM

Berlage, Herman Joseph. Incognito: a Greek tragedy in four acts. [New York?] 1908. 38 p. 16°.   NBL p.v.9, no.1

Bidwell, J. R. Under protest. A comedy in one act. Adapted from the Spanish. Boston: W. H. Baker & Co., 1896. 14 p. 12°. (Baker's edition of plays.)
NBL p.v.18, no.16

Bien, H. M. Easter eve; or, The "New Hagodoh Shel Pesach." A metrical family-feast service, consisting of a prologue and one character poem; including the old traditions, legends and melodies. Cincinnati: Bloch Publishing and Printing Co. 1886. 28 p., 1 pl. 8°.   *PKO

—— "Purim." Cincinnati: Bloch Pub. Co., 1889. 28 p. 2. ed. rev. 8°.   *PSQ

Binns, Henry Bryan. The adventure; a romantic variation on a Homeric theme. New York: B. W. Huebsch, 1911. 5 p.l., 96 p. 12°.   NBM

Bisbee, Noah, the younger. The history of the Falcos. A comedy in four acts. Walpole, N. H.: printed for the author at the Observatory Press, 1808. 137 p. 12°.
Reserve

Bitney, Mayme Riddle. The light brigade. A comic entertainment for ladies. Chicago: T. S. Denison [cop. 1908]. 22 p. 12°. (Denison's specialties.)
NBL p.v.8, no.15

—— The third degree. A burlesque initiation for women's societies, any order. Chicago: T. S. Denison [cop. 1907]. 15 p. 12°. (Denison's specialties.)
NBL p.v.8, no.17

Bixby, Frank L. The little boss. A comedy drama in four acts. Boston: W. H. Baker & Co., 1901. 44 p. 12°. (Baker's edition of plays.)   NBL p.v.14, no.2

Blair, Louisa Coleman, and R. F. WILLIAMS. Nathaniel Bacon, a play in four acts. Richmond, Virginia: The Hermitage Press, 1907. 3 p.l., 5–96 p., 3 pl. 8°.
NBL p.v.11, no.14

Blake, James Vila. A play in four acts The Lady Bertha's honeybroth, founded on Dumas' story of the same name. Chicago: Pryor Press, 1911. 144 p. 12°. NBM

Blashfield, Evangeline Wilbour. Masques of Cupid: A surprise party, The lesser evil, The honor of the Crequy, In Cleon's garden. Illustrations by E. H. Blashfield. New York: C. Scribner's Sons, 1901. viii p., 1 l., 264 p., 35 pl. 8°.   NBM

Blatt, William M. Husbands on approval; a comedy in three acts. Boston: W. H. Baker & Co., 1914. 197 p. 12°. NCR

Block, Henry William Charles. John Carver; a drama in five acts. Author's edition. [St. Louis, Mo., cop. 1902.] 286 p. 12°.   NBM

Block, Louis James. Capriccios. New York: G. P. Putnam's Sons, 1898. 1 p.l., ix, 130 p. 12°.   NBM
The birth and death of the prince. On the mountain top. At the foot of the rainbow. Myriad-minded man — an imaginary conversation. The day of days — a prothalamion.

—— Exile: a dramatic episode. St. Louis: G. I. Jones & Co., 1880. 120 p. 16°.
NBM

—— The judge; a play in four acts. Boston: Gorham Press [1915]. 5 p.l., 7–119 p. 12°. (American dramatists series.)
NBM

—— The world's triumph; a play, prologue — five acts — epilogue. Philadelphia: J. B. Lippincott Company, 1909. 165(1) p. 12°. **NBM**

The **Blockheads**; or, Fortunate contractor. An opera, in two acts, as it was performed at New York... Printed at New York. London, Re-printed for G. Kearsley, 1782. v p., 1 l., 43 p., 2 pl. 8°. **Reserve**

Boker, George Henry. Anne Boleyn: a tragedy. Philadelphia: A. Hart, 1850. viii, (i) 14–225 p. 12°. **NBM**

—— Calaynos: a tragedy. Philadelphia: E. H. Butler & Co., 1848. iv p., 1 l., 9–218 p. 2. ed. 12°. **NBM**

—— Königsmark, The legend of the hounds, and other poems. Philadelphia: J. B. Lippincott & Co., 1869. 244 p. 12°. **NBI**

Königsmark: a tragedy, p. 7–156.

—— Plays and poems. Boston: Ticknor & Fields, 1857. 2 v. 2. ed. 12°. **NBM**

v. 1. Calaynos. Anne Boleyn. Leonor de Guzman. Francesca da Rimini.
v. 2. The betrothal: a play. The widow's marriage: a comedy.

——The podesta's daughter, and other miscellaneous poems. Philadelphia: A. Hart, 1852. vi, 13–156 p. 12°. **NBI**

The podesta's daughter: a dramatic sketch, p. 13–52.

Boltwood, Edward. Balm of Gilead. A mixed foursome, in one act. New York: De Witt (1899). 18 p. 12°. (De Witt's acting plays. no. 412.) **NBL p.v.5, no.5**

Bostelmann, Lewis F. Roger of Rutland. A drama in four acts. n. t.-p. (New York: Fairchild Co., 1909?) 24 p. illus. f°. **†† NBF p.v.3, no.11**

—— Rutland; a chronologically arranged outline of the life of Roger Manners, fifth earl of Rutland, author of the works issued in folio in 1623 under the nom de plume "Shake-Speare," profusely illustrated; also a drama, showing the modus operandi of the engagement of William Shaxper of Stratford-on-Avon (2. ed.), as dummy and strawman for the earl-author, amended and greatly augmented, and the birth of the folio, showing how the great folio came into existence. New York: Rutland Publishing Company, 1911. 4 p.l., 3–186 p., 12 pl., 2 port. 8°. ***NCZ**

Botsford, Margaret. The reign of reform; or, Yankee Doodle court. By a lady (Margaret Botsford). Baltimore: printed for the authoress, 1830. iv, (1)6–146 p. 24°. **IO (1830)**

Boucicault, Dion.
Only the plays written during the author's residence in this country are included in this list.

The colleen bawn; or, The brides of Garryowen. A domestic drama, in three acts. London: T. H. Lacy (1860?). 52 p.

12°. (Lacy's acting edition of plays. v. 63.) **NCO**
The Library also has a prompter's copy, interleaved, and with ms. notes.

Grimaldi; or, The life of an actress. A drama, in five acts. New York, 1856. 36 p. 12°. **NCOF**
The Library has two prompter's copies of this edition, each interleaved, and with ms. notes.

Jessie Brown; or, The relief of Lucknow. A drama in three acts. New York: Samuel French, cop. 1858. 32 p. 12°. (Bourcicault's dramatic works. no. 6.) **NCO p.v.327, no.5**
The Library also has two prompter's copies of this edition, each interleaved, and with ms. notes.

—— —— London: T. H. Lacy (1858?) 38 p. 12°. (Lacy's acting edition of plays. v. 38.) **NCO**

"Led astray." A drama in 6 acts. (187–?) v. p. 8°. **†NCOF**
Manuscript promptbook, marked by the author.

The long strike. A drama, in four acts. New York: Samuel French, n.d. 38 p. 12°. (French's standard drama. no. 360.) **NCOF**
The Library has two prompter's copies, each interleaved and with ms. notes.

The octoroon; or, Life in Louisiana. A play, in four acts. London: T. H. Lacy (1861?). 43 p. 12°. (Lacy's acting edition of plays. v. 65.) **NCO**
The Library also has a prompter's copy of this edition, interleaved, and with ms. notes.

—— —— Printed, not published. n. p. n.d. 40 p. 12°. **NCOF**
Prompter's copy, interleaved, and with ms. notes.

Pauvrette. A drama in five acts. New York: Samuel French (1858). 36 p. 12°. (Bourcicault's dramatic works. no. 7.) **NCOF**
The Library has three prompter's copies, each interleaved, and with ms. notes.

The phantom. A drama, in two acts. New York: Samuel French, 1856. 28 p. 12°. (Bourcicault's dramatic works. no. 3. French's edition of standard dramas. no. 165.) **NBM p.v.2**
The Library also has a prompter's copy, interleaved, and with ms. notes.

The poor of New York. A drama in five acts. By the **** Club. (By Dion Boucicault.) New York: S. French (1857). 45 p. 12°. (French's standard drama. no. 189.) **NBM p.v.2**
The Library also has a prompter's copy, interleaved, and with ms. notes.

The Shaughraun. An original drama, in three acts. London: S. French (1875?) 64 p. 12°. (French's acting edition of plays. v. 123.) **NCO**
The Library also has a prompter's copy of this edition, interleaved, and with ms. notes.

—— —— n. p., n.d. 22 p., 23 f., 22 p. 8° **NCOF**
Prompter's copy, interleaved, and with ms. notes.

Bowman, James Cloyd. The gift of white roses. ⌈Drama, in verse.⌉ Ada, O.: University Herald Press ⌈1913⌉. 76 p. 2. ed. 12°.   **NBM**

—— Into the depths. (A story of protecting sympathy.) Together with sixteen miscellaneous poems. ⌈Valparaiso, Ind.: University Press, 1905. 112 p. 12°.   **NBI**

Boyd, Jackson. The unveiling; a poetic drama in five acts. New York: G. P. Putnam's Sons, 1915. vii, 255 p., 1 port. 12°.   **NBM**

Brackenridge, Hugh Henry. The Battle of Bunker's-Hill. A Dramatic Piece of Five Acts, in heroic measure; by a Gentleman of Maryland... Philadelphia: Printed and sold by Robert Bell, 1776. 3 p.l., (1)6-49(1) p., 1 pl. 8°.   **Reserve**
Library copy lacks the title-page. Title taken from Wegelin's *Early American plays.*

—— The Death of General Montgomery, at the Siege of Quebec. A tragedy. With an Ode, in honour of the Pennsylvania Militia, and the small band of regular Continental Troops, who sustained the Campaign, in the depth of winter, January, 1777, and repulsed the British Forces from the Banks of the Delaware. By the Author of a Dramatic Piece on the Battle of Bunker's-Hill. To which are added, Elegiac Pieces, commemorative of distinguished Characters... Philadelphia: Printed and Sold by Robert Bell, 1777. 79(1) p., 2 l., 1 pl. 8°.   **Reserve**

—— The Death of General Montgomery, in storming the City of Quebec. A Tragedy. ⌈Remainder of title same as previous entry.⌉ Norwich: Printed by J. Trumbull, 1777. 68 p. 8°.   **Reserve**

Brackett, Charles William. Jocelyn: a play, and thirty verses. Boston: Richard G. Badger ⌈cop. 1915⌉. 93 p. 12°.   **NBM**
Jocelyn: a play, p. 9–45.

Braeunlich, Herman. Columbus. Historical play in four acts. New York: H. Braeunlich & Co. ⌈cop. 1904.⌉ 58 p. 16°.   **NBM**

Brandreth, Paulina. Plays and poems. New York: Broadway Publishing Co. ⌈1910.⌉ 119 p. 12°.   **NBI**
The plays included are The poet's vision and Maretta.

Brazza-Savorgnan, Cora A. Slocomb, contessa di. A literary farce. Boston: The Arena Pub. Co., 1896. 2 p.l., 36 p. 4°.   **NBL p.v.10, no.1**

Breck, Charles. The fox chase. A comedy in five acts. New York: D. Longworth, 1808. 64 p. 16°.   **NCO p.v.246, no.4**

—— The trust. A comedy in five acts. ⌈In verse.⌉ New York: D. Longworth, 1808. 82 p. 16°.   **NCO p.v.249, no.2**

Breck, Joseph. West Point; or, A tale of treason. An historical drama, in three acts. Dramatised from Ingraham's Romance of American history. With a prologue by J. H. Hewitt, epiloque by R. H. Pratt. Baltimore: Bull & Tuttle, 1840. 22 p. 12°.   **NBL p.v.21, no.4**

Brewster, Emma E. Aunt Mehetible's scientific experiment. A farce in one act. Boston: W. H. Baker & Co., 1901. 11 p. 12°. (Baker's edition of plays.)   **NBL p.v.19, no.18**

Brinton, Daniel Garrison. Maria Candelaria. An historic drama from American aboriginal life. Philadelphia: D. McKay. 1897. xxix, 98 p., 2 pl. 12°.   **HB**

Briscoe, Margaret Sutton. The frog fairy. A play in three acts. (In: Harper's book of little plays ⌈for children⌉. New York, 1910. 12°. p. 1–20.)   **NBL**

Broadhurst, George H. What happened to Jones: an original farce in three acts. New York: S. French, 1910. 107 p. 12°. (French's standard library edition.) **NBM**

Brock, Howard Folsom. The bank account. ⌈A one act tragedy.⌉ (Harvard monthly. Cambridge, Mass., 1914. 8°. v. 58, p. 33–50.)   **STG**

Brooke, Van Dyke. The quicksands of Gotham. A drama in prologue and three acts. Boston: W. H. Baker & Co., 1899. 43 p. 12°. (Baker's edition of plays.)   **NBL p.v.19, no.17**

Brougham, John.
Only the plays written during the author's residence in this country are included in this list.

Columbus el filibustero. A...⌈comedy⌉. New York: S. French ⌈1858⌉. 24 p. 12°. (The minor drama. no. 145.)   **NBM p.v.2**

David Copperfield. A drama, in two acts. Adapted from Dickens'...work of the same name. New York: S. French ⌈18—?⌉. 24 p. 12°. (French's American drama. no. 18.)   **NCO p.v.324, no.4**

A decided case. A dramatic sketch, in one act. New York: S. French ⌈cop. 1857⌉. 18 p. 12°. (The minor drama. no. 114.)   **NCO p.v.268, no.9**

The demon lover; or, My cousin german: a romantic comedietta, in two acts. New York: S. French ⌈1856⌉. 26 p. 12°. (French's minor drama. no. 105.)   **NBM p.v.2**

Dombey and Son. Dramatized from Dickens' novel. In three acts. New York: S. French, n. d. 31 p. 12°. (French's American drama. no. 126.)   **NBM p.v.2**

Dred; or, The Dismal Swamp. A play, in five acts...from Mrs. H. B. Stowe's novel. New York: S. French ⌈1856⌉. 43 p. 12°. (French's American drama. no. 100.)   **NBM p.v.2**

Brougham, John, continued.

Flies in the web. An original comedy ... London: T. H. Lacy [cop. 1860]. 50 p. 12°. (Lacy's acting edition of plays. v. 69.) **NCO**

The game of life. An original comedy. New York: S. French, cop. 1856. 44 p. 12°. (French's American drama; the acting edition. no. 116.) **NCOF**

The game of love. An original comedy, in five acts. New York: S. French, cop. 1855. 54 p. 12°. (French's American drama; acting edition. no. 105.) **NCOF**

The gun-maker of Moscow: melodrama, in three acts. New York: S. French [1856]. 28 p. 12°. (French's standard drama. no. 164.) **NBM p.v.2**

The lottery of life; a story of New York. An original local drama in five acts. London: S. French [18—?]. 42 p. 12°. (French's acting edition of plays. v. 105.) **NCO**

Much ado about a Merchant of Venice, — from the original text — a long way. New York: S. French, 1868. 24 p. 12°. (French's minor drama. no. 308.) **NCOF**

Playing with fire. An original comedy, in five acts. London: T. H. Lacy [1861]. 58 p. 12°. (Lacy's acting edition of plays. v. 66.) **NCO**

Po-ca-hon-tas; or, The gentle savage. [An extravaganza.] New York: S. French, n.d. 32 p. 12°. (French's American drama; acting edition. no. 69.) **NCOF**
Prompter's copy; interleaved with ms. notes.
Reprinted in Alfred Bates, *The drama*, v. 20, p. 153–195.

The red mask; or, The wolf of Lithuania. A melo-drama, in three acts. New York: S. French [1856]. 26 p. 12°. French's standard drama. no. 158.) **NBM p.v.2**

Temptation; or, The Irish emigrant. A comic drama, in two acts. New York: S. French, cop. 1856. 22 p. 12°. (French's American drama; acting edition. no. 65.) **NCOF**
Prompter's copy, interleaved. With ms. notes.

Brown, Alice. Children of earth; a play of New England. New York: Macmillan Co., 1915. 7 p.l., 212 p., 1 port. 12°. **NBM**

Brown, Charles Brockden. Alcuin; a dialogue. New-York: Printed by T. & J. Swords, 1798. 77 p. 12°. **Reserve**

Brown, Charles Hovey. Moses: a drama. Boston: Gorham Press, 1902. 69 p. 8°. ***PSQ**

Brown, David Paul. Sertorius: or, The Roman patriot. A tragedy. Philadelphia: E. L. Carey & A. Hart, 1830. 87 p. 8°. **NBM**

Brown, J. H. Katrina's little game. A Dutch act, with songs and a dance... New York: R. M. De Witt, 1876. 8 p. 12°. (De Witt's Ethiopian and comic drama. no. 103.) **NBL p.v.18, no.22**

Brown, S. J. In the enemy's camp: or, The stolen despatches. A drama in three acts. Boston: W. H. Baker & Co. [cop. 1889.] 33 p. 12°. (Baker's edition of plays.) **NBL p.v.11, no.1**

Browne, F. E. Ruth: a sacred drama. and original lyrical poems. New York: Wynkoop & Hallenbeck, 1871. 2 p.l., vii–viii, 121 p. 12°. **NBI**

Browne, Walter. Everywoman; her pilgrimage in quest of love. A modern morality play. New York: The H. K. Fly Company [1911]. 5 p.l., (1)8–121 p., 8 pl. 12°. **NBM**

Browne, William Maynadier. The trustee. A play in four acts. Boston: W. H. Baker & Co. [cop. 1891.] 38 p. 12°. (Baker's edition of plays.) **NBL p.v.18, no.18**

Brownell, Atherton. The unseen empire; a peace play in four acts... [With introduction by D. S. Jordan.] New York: Harper & Bros., 1914. 2 p.l., iii–iv p., 2 l., 176 p., 1 l. 8°. **NBM**

Bugbee, Willis N. The new pastor; a vaudeville sketch in one act. New York: Dick & Fitzgerald, 1912. 12 p. 12°. **NBL p.v.27, no.8**

—— A rustic minstrel show; an entertainment in one act. New York: Dick & Fitzgerald, 1912. 29 p. 12°. **NBL p.v.27, no.6**

Bunge, Martin Ludwig Detloff. Abraham Lincoln; a historical drama in four acts. Milwaukee. Wis.: Co-operative Printery [cop. 1911]. 38 p. 24°. **NBL p.v.31, no.1**

Burk, John Daly. Bethlem Gabor, lord of Transylvania, or, The man hating palatine; an historical drama, in three acts. Petersburg: printed by J. Dickson, for Somervell & Conrad, 1807. 49 p. 16°. **NCR p.v.8**

—— Bunker-Hill; or, The death of General Warren: an historic tragedy, in five acts. New York: D. Longworth, 1817. 44 p. 16°. **NCO p.v.250, no.4**

—— —— With an introductory essay by Brander Matthews. New York: The Dunlap Society, 1891. 4 p.l., 82 p., 1 pl. 8°. (Dunlap Society. Publications. no. 15.) **NBL (Dunlap)**

—— Female patriotism; or, The death of Joan d'Arc. An historic play in five acts. New York, 1798. 40 p. 12°. **NBM p.v.5**
Title-page lacking; title taken from Oscar Wegelin's *Early American plays.*

Burke, Charles. Rip Van Winkle: a legend of the Catskills. A romantic drama, in two acts. Adapted from Washington

Irving's Sketch book by Charles Burke. (Reprinted in: Alfred Bates, editor, The drama. London, 1903. 8°. v. 19, p. 299–336.)   **NAF**

Burnett, J. G. Blanche of Brandywine. An American patriotic spectacle... New York: S. French ₁cop. 1858₁. 40 p. 12°. (French's standard drama: acting edition. no. 206.)   **NCOF**
By the dead waters. In the mist. The throne-room. The walled garden. The shrine.

Burr, Amelia J. Plays in the market-place. Englewood, N. J.: The Hillside Press, 1910. 4 p.l., 7–74 p., 1 l. 8°.   **NBM**
By the dead waters. In the mist. The throne-room. The walled garden. The shrine.

—— The point of life. A play in three acts. Englewood, N. J.: The Hillside Press, 1907. 3 p.l., 6–88 p., 1 l. 8°. **NBM**

Burton, Mrs. H. S. Don Quixote de la Mancha. A comedy in five acts, taken from Cervantes' novel of that name. San Francisco: J. H. Carmany & Co., 1876. 63 p. 12°.   **NBL p.v.19, no.14**

Burton, Lena Dalkeith. Everychild; morality play, by Lena D. Burton, in co-operation with Marian K. Brown. ₁In verse.₁ Boston: C. W. Thompson & Co., 1911. 7 l., 1 pl. 8°.   **NBL p.v.29, no.13**

Burton, Richard. Rahab. A drama in three acts. New York: Henry Holt & Co., 1906. 4 p.l., 5–119 p. 8°.   ***PSQ**

Burton, William Evans. Ellen Wareham, the wife of two husbands. A domestic drama in two acts... London: T. H. Lacy ₁1833₁. 36 p. 12°. (Lacy's acting edition of plays. v. 34.)   **NCO**

Bush, Thomas. Santiago, a drama, in five acts. Toronto ₁18—?₁. 55 p., 1 l. 8°.   *** C p.v.613**

Byars, William Vincent. The house of fate. A soothsaying of liberty. ₁Drama, in verse.₁ ₁New York? 19—?₁ 36 p. 12°.   **NBL p.v.9, no.2**

Bynner, Witter. The little king; a play in one act. (Forum. New York, 1914. 8°. v. 51, p. 605–632.)   ***DA**

—— Tiger; a one act play. (Forum. New York, 1913. 8°. v. 49, p. 522–547.)   ***DA**

Callaway, Emilie H. A widow's wiles: a comedy in three acts. New York: Dick & Fitzgerald, cop. 1908. 34 p. 12°.
                            NBL p.v.7, no.22

Calvert, George Henry. Arnold and André. An historical drama. Boston: Little, Brown and Company, 1864. xv, (1)18–95 p. 12°.   **NBM**

—— —— Boston: Lee and Shepard. 1876. xv, (1)18–95 p. new ed. 12°. **NBM**

—— Brangonar. A tragedy. Boston: Lee and Shepard ₁1883₁. 110 p. 12°.
                            NBM

—— Comedies. Boston: Phillips, Sampson & Co., 1856. 125 p. 8°.   **NBM**
The will and the way. Like unto like.

—— Count Julian. A tragedy. Baltimore: M. Hickman, 1840. 69 p. 12°.
                            NBM p.v.4

—— The maid of Orleans; an historical tragedy. New York: G. P. Putnam's Sons, 1874. 134 p. 12°.   **NBM**

—— Mirabeau. An historical drama. Boston: Lee & Shepard ₁1883₁. 3 p.l., (1) 8–103 p. 16°.   **NBM**

Cameron, Margaret. The teeth of the gift horse. New York: S. French, cop. 1909. 31 p. 12°. (French's acting edition of plays. v. 157.)   **NCO**

Campbell, Marian D. A Chinese dummy. A farce in one act. For female characters only... Boston: W. H. Baker & Co. ₁cop. 1899.₁ 17 p. 12°. (Baker's edition of plays.)   **NBL p.v.18, no.20**

Campbell, William Wilfred. Mordred and Hildebrand. A book of tragedies. ₁In verse.₁ Ottawa: J. Durie & Son, 1895. 3 p.l., 168 p. 16°.   **NCR**

Cannon, Charles James. Dramas. New York: E. Dunigan & Bro., 1857. 355 p. 12°.   **NBM**
The sculptor's daughter. Dolores. Better late than never. The oath of office.

Carb, David. The new age. (Harvard monthly. Cambridge, Mass., 1910. 8°. v. 50, no. 3, May, 1910, p. 7–20.)   **STG**

—— The voice of the people; a play in three acts. Boston: Four Seas Co., 1912. 2 p.l., 129 p. 12°.   **NBM**

Carleton, Henry Guy. Memnon. A tragedy in five acts. ₁Chicago:₁ printed, not published ₁1881₁. 171 p. 12°.   **NBM**

Carleton, John L. Coom-na-goppel. A drama in five acts for male characters only. Chicago and New York: The Dramatic Publishing Company, cop. 1906. 51 p. 12°. (Sergel's acting drama. no. 581.)   **NBL p.v.4, no.11**

—— More sinned against than sinning. An original Irish drama, in a prologue and three acts. Chicago: The Dramatic Publishing Company, cop. 1883. 26 p. 12°. (American acting drama.)
                            NBL p.v.17, no.20

Carpenter, Rhys. The tragedy of Etarre; a poem. ₁In four acts and in verse.₁ New York: Sturgis & Walton, 1912. v, 137(1) p. 12°.   **NBM**

Carus, Paul. The Buddha; a drama in three acts and four interludes. ₁In verse.₁ Chicago: The Open Court Publishing Co., 1911. iv, 68 p. 12°.   **NBM**

—— K'ung Fu Tze. A dramatic poem. Chicago: The Open Court Publishing Co., 1915. 1 p.l., (1)6–72 p. 8°.   **NBM**

Castle, Harriet D. The courting of Mother Goose. An entertainment. n. t.-p. n. p. ₁188–?₁ 27 p. 12°. **NBL p.v.17, no.21**

Catharine Brown, the converted Cherokee: a missionary drama, founded on fact. By a lady. New-Haven: S. Converse, prtr., 1819. 27 p. 8°. **HBC**

Caverly, Robert Boodey. The regicides (N. E.). An historical drama. (Years 1640–1676.) Boston: published by the author, 1884. 2 p.l., 193–247 p. 8°. **HBC**

Cawein, Madison Julius. The shadow garden (a phantasy) and other plays. New York: G. P. Putnam's Sons, 1910. v, 259 p. 12°. **NBM**
The shadow garden, a phantasy. The house of fear, a mystery. The witch, a miracle. Cabestaing, a tragedy in three acts.

Chandos, C. M. Ruby. Drama, in three acts. New York, 1874. 3 p.l., 5–67 p. 8°. **NBM**

Chapman, John Jay. Homeric scenes; Hector's farewell and The wrath of Achilles. New York: L. J. Gomme, 1914. 4 p.l., (1)8–76 p. 16°. **NBM**

—— The maid's forgiveness. A play. New York: Moffat, Yard & Co., 1908. 3 p.l., 93(1) p., 1 l. 12°. **NBM**

—— A sausage from Bologna: a comedy in four acts. New York: Moffat, Yard & Co., 1909. 4 p.l., 113(1) p. 12°. **NBM**

—— The treason & death of Benedict Arnold; a play for a Greek theatre. ₁New York:₁ Moffat, Yard & Company, 1910. 76 p. 8°. **NBM**

Chase, F. E. The great umbrella case. A mock trial. Boston: W. H. Baker & Co. ₁cop. 1889.₁ 36 p. new ed. 12°. (Baker's edition of plays.) **NBL p.v.5, no.18**

Cheney, John Vance. Queen Helen, and other poems. Chicago: Way & Williams, 1895. 4 p.l., 78 p. 12°. **NBI**
Queen Helen, p. 1–52.

The **Church** and the stage, and the new religious drama, "The ninety and nine," written by Ramsay Morris, founded on the theme of Ira D. Sankey's famous hymn, to be presented at the Academy of Music in New York City in October, 1902. Production by Frank McKee. ₁New York,₁ 1902. 8 l. 16°. **NBL p.v.27, no.16**

Churchill, Winston. The title-mart. A comedy in three acts. New York: The Macmillan Co., 1905. 3 p.l., 215 p. 12°. **NBM**

Cinderella. An accurate description of the grand allegorical pantomimic spectacle of Cinderella; or, The little glass slipper. New York: W. Turner, 1808. 24 p. 16°. **NBM p.v.7**

Clark, Samuel N. The delegates from Denver: a farcical comedy in two acts. New York: Dick & Fitzgerald, cop. 1908. 21 p. 12°. **NBL p.v.7, no.21**

Clark, William M. The parson's perversity. A comedy in three acts. Philadelphia: Penn Pub. Co., 1907. 24 p. 12°. **NBL p.v.8, no.8**

Clarke, George. The doctor. In four acts. ₁With separate part of one of the characters in the play.₁ ₁New York, 1912?₁ 5 parts. 4°. **Reserve**
Typewritten.

Clarke, Helen Archibald. Balaustion's Euripides: a dramatic version of 'Balaustion's adventure' and 'Aristophanes' apology' ₁by Robert Browning₁ made for the Boston Browning Society by Helen Archibald Clarke. (Poet lore. Boston, 1915. 8°. v. 26, p. 1–46.) ***DA**

Clinch, Charles Powell. The spy; a tale of the neutral ground. From the novel of that name ₁by James Fenimore Cooper₁. A dramatic romance. In three acts. ₁By C. P. Clinch.₁ 1822. 2 p.l., 82 p., 3 l. 8°. **NCOF**
Manuscript promptbook.

Cockings, George. The Conquest of Canada; or, The Siege of Quebec. An historical tragedy of five acts. London: Printed for the Author; and sold by J. Cooke ₁and others₁, MDCCLXVI. 1 p.l., v(i), 76 p. 8°. **Reserve**

Collyer, Dan. Christmas eve in the South; or, Uncle Caleb's home. An Ethiopian farce, in one act and five scenes. New York: The Dramatic Publishing Company, cop. 1882. 8 p. 12°. (De Witt's Ethiopian and comic drama. no. 148.) **NBL p.v.16, no.20**

Columbus, the great discoverer of America. A drama in five acts. By an Ursuline. New York: Benziger Bros., vii, 3–55 p., 1 port. 16°. **NBM p.v.3**

Comfort, Richard. Nero. A tragedy. Philadelphia, 1880. 94 p. 1 l., 1 pl. 16°. **NBM**

Congdon, James B. Quaker quiddities; or, Friends in council. A colloquy. Boston: Crosby, Nichols, Lee & Co., 1860. 48 p. 12°. **NBM**
Published anonymously.

Conrad, Robert Taylor. Jack Cade. ₁A drama in five acts, in verse. Text of the play, with the parts of the different characters.₁ 2 v. 12°. **NCOF**
Manuscript promptbook.

—— Jack Cade, the captain of the commons. A tragedy. In four acts. With an historical introduction. London: T. H. Lavy ₁1868₁. 65(1) p. 12°. (Lacy's acting edition of plays. v. 83.) **NCO**

Conway, H. J. Dred: a tale of the Great Dismal Swamp. A drama in four acts, founded on the novel of the same title by Mrs. H. B. Stowe. New York: J. W. Amerman, 1856. 46 p. 12°.   **NCOF**

Prompter's copy, interleaved. With ms. notes.

Cook, S. N. Broken promises. A temperance drama, in five acts. New York: Happy Hours Company, cop. 1879. vi, (1)8–41 p. 12°.   **NCO p.v.301, no.16**

Coon, Hilton. The widow from the West: or, The late Mr. Early. A farce comedy in three acts. Boston: W. H. Baker & Co., 1898. 26 p. 12°. (Baker's edition of plays.)   **NBL p.v.5, no.17**

Corbin, John. Husband, and The forbidden guests: two plays. Boston: Houghton Mifflin Co., 1910. xxxiii p., 5 l., (1) 10–271(1) p. 12°.   **NBM**

Cotter, Joseph Seamon. Caleb, the degenerate, a play in four acts. A study of the types, customs, and needs of the American negro. Louisville, Ky.: The Bradley & Gilbert Co., 1903. 57 p., 1 port. 8°.   **NBL p.v.24, no.2**

Coughlan, Arthur T. The prophecy; a play [in three acts] of the days of persecution under Henry VIII. of England. (For male characters.) Northeast, Pa.: St. Mary's College [1911]. 68 p. 16°.   **NBL p.v.13, no.1**

Cowan, Sada. The state forbids; a play in one act. New York: M. Kennerley, 1915. 46 p. 12°.   **NBM**

Cowles, Florence A. Where the lane turned; a rural comedy drama in four acts. New York: Dick & Fitzgerald, 1912. 53 p. 12°.   **NBL p.v.27, no.14**

Cowley, E. J. The Bohemians. A comedy in three acts. Boston: W. H. Baker & Co. [cop. 1896.] 43 p. 12°. (Baker's edition of plays.)   **NBL p.v.17, no.1**

Cox, Ethel Louise. Poems, lyric and dramatic. Boston: Richard G. Badger, 1904. vi, 195 p. 12°.   **NBI**

The combat with the dragon, p. 177–195.

Coxe, Arthur Cleveland. Saul, a mystery. New York: D. Appleton & Co., 1845. x p., 1 l., (1)14–297(1) p. 12°.   **NBM**

Crafts, William. The sea serpent; or, Gloucester hoax. A dramatic jeu d'esprit, in three acts. Charleston: A. E. Miller, 1819. 34 p. 12°.   **NBM p.v.6**

Craigie, Pearl Mary Teresa Richards. Osbern and Ursyne. A drama in three acts, by John Oliver Hobbes [pseud.]. London: John Lane, 1900. 4 p.l., 94 p., 1 l. 8°.   **NCR**

—— The wisdom of the wise; a comedy in three acts [by John Oliver Hobbes, pseud.]. New York: F. A. Stokes Co. [1900.] 4 p.l., 136 p. 12°. **NCO p.v.314, no.11**

Cranch, Christopher Pearse. Satan: a libretto. Boston: Roberts Bros., 1874. 36 p. 16°.   **NBM**

Crane, Eleanor Maud. A little savage. A military comedy in three acts. New York: Dick & Fitzgerald, 1907. 50 p. 12°.   **NBL p.v.7, no.18**

—— Next door. A comedy of to-day. New York: Dick & Fitzgerald [1906]. 63 p. 12°.   **NBL p.v.1, no.1**

—— The rainbow kimona. A comedy in two acts for girls. New York: Dick & Fitzgerald, 1908. 33 p. 12°.   **NBL p.v.7, no.16**

Crane, Elizabeth G. Berquin. A drama in five acts. New York: Charles Scribner's Sons, 1897. vi p., 1 l., 110 p. 12°.   **NBL p.v.23, no.4**

—— The imperial republic. A drama of the day. New York: Grafton Press [cop. 1902]. 2 p.l., 122 p. 12°.   **NBM**

—— The necken; an original play in two acts [and in verse]. New York, 1913. 73 p. 12°.   **NBL p.v.30, no.6**

Crawford, J. R. Lovely Peggy; a play in three acts based on the love romance of Margaret Woffington and David Garrick. New Haven: Yale University Press, 1911. 4 p.l., (1)4–173 p. 8°.   **NBM**

—— Robin of Sherwood; a comedy in three acts and four scenes. [In verse.] New Haven: Yale University Press, 1912. 5 p.l., 7–150 p. 8°.   **NBM**

Creamer, Edward S. The Orphean tragedy. [In verse.] New York: The Abbey Press [cop. 1901]. 153 p. 8°.   **NBM**

Creevey, Caroline A., and MARGARET E. SANGSTER. The Ninepin Club; or, Flora, the queen of summer. (In: Harper's book of little plays [for children]. New York, 1910. 12°. p. 53–73.)   **NBL**

—— A Thanksgiving dream. (In: Harper's book of little plays [for children]. New York, 1910. 12°. p. 121–142.)   **NBL**

Crigler, John Fielding. Saul of Tarsus; a religious drama [in 7 acts and in verse]. Boston: Sherman, French & Co., 1914. 5 p.l., 226 p. 12°.   **NBM**

Crippen, T. G. Joseph in Egypt. A Biblical drama in five acts. Edited by C. J. Hanssen. New York: The Dramatic Publishing Company [18—?]. 28 p. 16°. (The wizard series.)   ***PSQ**

Cronkhite, H. M. Reymond: a drama of the American revolution. New York: G. P. Putnam's Sons, 1886. 101 p. 12°. **NBM**

Crothers, Rachel. A man's world; a play in four acts. Boston: R. G. Badger [1915]. 2 p.l., 7–113 p. 12°. (American dramatists series.)   **NBM**

Crow, Martha Foote. The world above. A duologue. Chicago: The Blue Sky Press [cop. 1905]. 2 p.l., 7–37 p. 8°. **NBM**
no. 209 of 500 copies printed.

Crowe, S. The comedy of fraud. An American drama. One act. One scene. [New York,] 1895. 63 p. 16°. **NBM**

—— The merchant prince. One act. One scene. [New York,] 1895. 63 p. 16°. **NBM**

Curtis, Arriana Randolph Wormeley. The coming woman; or, The spirit of seventy-six. A prophetic drama. London: S. French [186–?]. 28 p. 12°. (French's acting edition of plays. v. 112.) **NCO**

—— The spirit of seventy-six; or, The coming woman. A prophetic drama, followed by A change of base and Doctor Mondschein. Boston: Little, Brown & Co., 1868. 141 p. 12°. **NBM**

—— —— Boston: Little, Brown & Co., 1869. 141 p. 8. ed. 12°. **NBM**

Curtis, H. P. Uncle Robert; or, Love's labor saved. A comedy. In three acts. Boston: W. H. Baker & Co. [cop. 1861.] 34 p. 12°. (Baker's edition of plays.) **NBL p.v.15, no.9**

Cushing, Charles C. S. Nathan Hale of '73. A drama in four acts. New Haven: Yale Publishing Association, 1908. 2 p.l., vii–x, 88 p., 1 l., 7 pl., 1 port. 8°. **NBM**
no. 341 of 500 copies printed.

Custis, George Washington Parke. Pocahontas; or, The settlers of Virginia. A national drama in three acts. Philadelphia: C. Alexander, 1830. 47 p. 12°. **NBM**

Cutting, Arolyn Caverly. Rosemary; a comedy in four acts. New York: Dick & Fitzgerald, 1912. 35 p. 12°.
NBL p.v.27, no.11

Dale, H. C. A white lie. An original comedy drama in four acts. New York: H. Roorbach, 1899. 44 p. 12°.
NBL p.v.11, no.4

Dallas, Mary Kyle. Our Aunt Robertina. A comedietta in one act. Boston: W. H. Baker & Co., 1902. 12 p. 12°. (Baker's edition of plays.)
NBL p.v.17, no.3

Dalrymple, C. Leona. Mrs. Forrester's crusade; a farce in one act. New York: Dick & Fitzgerald [1911]. 8 p. 12°.
NBL p.v.17, no.6

—— Surprises. A farce in one act. New York: Dick & Fitzgerald, 1908. 17 p. 12°.
NBL p.v.7, no.17

—— Tangles; a farce in one act. New York: Dick & Fitzgerald, 1907. 18 p. 12°.
NBL p.v.7, no.20

—— A white shawl. A farce comedy in two acts. New York: Dick & Fitzgerald [1905]. 25 p. 12°. **NBL p.v.1, no.2**

Daly, Augustin. As you like it. A comedy by William Shakspere as arranged by Augustin Daly. First produced at Daly's theatre Dec. 17, 1889, and here printed from the prompter's copy. With a few introductory words by William Winter. New York: privately printed for Mr. Daly, 1890. 8°. *** NCN**

—— "Frou Frou;" a comedy of powerful human interest, in five acts, by Augustin Daly. New York: Samuel French, cop. 1870. 2 p.l., (1)4–59 p. 12°. (French's standard drama. no. 359.) **NCOF**
A translation of Meilhac's play.
The Library has two prompter's copies of this edition, each interleaved, and with ms. notes.

—— Love's labor's lost. A comedy written by William Shakspere. Arranged...for the present stage by Augustin Daly... With a few prefatory thoughts...by William Winter. New York: privately printed for Mr. Daly, 1891. 64 p. 8°.
* NCN p.v.5, no.9

—— Shakespeare's comedy of The merry wives of Windsor. A fac-simile in photolithography of the first quarto (1602). Together with a reprint of the prompt-copy prepared for use at Daly's theatre. The alterations and emendations by Augustin Daly. To which is added an introduction by William Winter. New York: printed for Mr. Daly, 1886. xi p., 1 l., 2–53, 72 p. 8°. ***NCMB**

—— Taming of the shrew. A comedy... as arranged by Augustin Daly. With an introduction by William Winter... New York: privately printed for Mr. Daly, 1887. 75 p., 6 ms. sheets of music, 1 port. 8°. *** NCP**
Prompter's copy, interleaved; with ms. notes.

—— Under the gaslight; or, Life and love in these times: an original drama of American life, in four acts. London: T. H. Lacy [18–?]. 60 p. 12°. (Lacy's acting edition of plays. v. 81.) **NCO**

—— Under the gaslight: a totally original and picturesque drama of love in these times, in five acts. Author's edition. New York: W. C. Wemyss, 1867. 47 p. 12° (Wemyss' acting drama.) **NCOF**
Prompter's copy, interleaved. With ms. notes.

—— —— New York: printed for the author, 1867. 93 p. 4°. **NCOF**
Leaves printed on one side only
Prompter's copy, with ms. notes.

—— —— [New York? 18—?] 1 p.l., 5–93 p. 4°. **NCOF**
Leaves printed on one side only.
Prompter's copy, with ms. notes.

Dargan, Olive Tilford. Lords and lovers, and other dramas. New York: Charles Scribner's Sons, 1906. 3 p.l., 315 p. 8°. **NBI**
Lords and lovers. The shepherd. The siege.

—— The mortal gods, and other plays. New York: Charles Scribner's Sons, 1912. 4 p.l., 3–303 p. 8°.   **NBM**

The mortal gods. A son of Hermes. Kidmir.

—— Semiramis, and other plays. New York: Brentano's, 1904. 1 p.l., 255 p. 8°.   **NBM**

Semiramis. Carlotta. The poet.

Darusmont, Frances Wright. Altorf. A tragedy. Philadelphia: M. Carey & Son, 1819. v p., 2 l., 5–83 p. 12°. **NBM p.v.6**

Davidson, Robert. Elijah, a sacred drama, and other poems. New York: Charles Scribner, 1860. 184 p. 12°. **NBI**

Elijah, p. 7–69.

Davis, Allan. The promised land: a drama in four acts. Cambridge: The Harvard Dramatic Club, 1908. 6 p.l., (1)12–69 p., 1 pl. 8°.   **NBL p.v.13, no.10**

Davis, Richard Harding. Farces: The dictator; The galloper; "Miss Civilization." New York: Charles Scribner's Sons, 1906. viii, 332 p., 16 pl., 2 port. 8°.   **NBM**

Dawes, Rufus. Athenia of Damascus. A tragedy. New York: S. Colman. 1839. 118 p., 1 pl. 12°. (Colman's dramatic library.)   **NBM p.v.3**

—— The battle of Stillwater; or, The maniac. In three acts, founded on national events, by the author of Pirate of the East [i. e., Rufus Dawes]. [1840?] 3 v. 8°.   **NCOF**

Manuscript promptbook.

—— Geraldine, Athenia of Damascus, and miscellaneous poems. New-York: Samuel Colman, 1839. 5 p.l., (1)16–343 p., 1 port. 12°.   **NBHD**

Athenia of Damascus: a tragedy, p. 113–201.

Day, Richard Edwin. Thor: a drama [in four acts] representative of human history. Syracuse, N. Y.: J. T. Roberts, 1880. 37 p. 16°.   **NBL p.v.12, no.1**

Dean, Frank J. Joe Ruggles; or, The girl miner. A comedy-drama, in four acts. Chicago: The Dramatic Pub. Co., cop. 1895. 29 p. 12°. (Sergel's acting drama. no. 404.)   **NBL p.v.4, no.13**

Delano, Mortimer. Out of the vast unknown depths. A phantom in one act. [New York: C. H. Eagle, 1908.] 12 p. 8°.   **NBL p.v. 10, no.4**

Dell, Floyd. A long time ago; a fantasy. (Forum. New York, 1914. 8°. v. 51, p. 261–277.)   ***DA**

D'Elville, Rinallo. The rescue; or, The villain unmasked. A farce, in three acts. New York: printed for the author, 1813. 44 p. 12°.   **NBM p.v.6**

Dement, Richmond Sheffield. Napoleon; a drama. Reading edition, with appendix. Chicago: Knight, Leonard & Co., 1893. 2 p.l., (1)10–183 p., 4 pl., 5 port. 12°.   **NBM**

Demuth, Charles. The azure adder. [A drama.] New York: A. and C. Boni, 1913. 31 p. 12°.   **NBL p.v.32, no.12**

De Peyster, John Watts. Bothwell... An historical drama. New York: C. H. Ludwig, 1884. 96 p., 1 port. 4°.   **NBM**

—— A charade or parlor drama. A night with Charles XII. of Sweden; or, A soldier's wife's fidelity. n. t.-p. [185–?] 12 p. 8°.   ***C p.v.1300, no.5**

Deseret deserted. [Drama in three acts.] [New York? 18—?] 3–28 p. 12°. **NCOF** Prompter's copy, mounted. Title-page missing.

Deutsch, Gotthard. Israel Bruna: an historical tragedy in five acts. Boston: R. G. Badger, 1908. 95 p. 12°. ***PSQ**

A **Dialogue,** between A Southern Delegate, and His Spouse, on his return from The Grand Continental Congress. A Fragment, inscribed To the Married Ladies of America... Printed in the Year MDCCLXXIV. 14 p. 8°.   **Reserve**

Dickinson, Thomas Herbert. In hospital. (In: T. H. Dickinson, editor, Wisconsin plays. New York, 1914. 12°. p. 69–112.)   **NBL**

—— Wisconsin plays, Thomas H. Dickinson, editor; original one-act plays from the repertory of the Wisconsin Dramatic Society [by] Zona Gale, Thomas H. Dickinson, William Ellery Leonard. New York: B. W. Huebsch, 1914. 7 p.l., 5–187 p. 12°.   **NBL**

The neighbours, by Zona Gale. In hospital, by T. H. Dickinson. Glory of the morning, by W. E. Leonard.

Dillaye, Ina. Ramona; a play in five acts, adapted from Helen Hunt Jackson's Indian novel. Syracuse, N. Y.: F. Le C. Dillaye, cop. 1887. 40 p. 12°.   **NBM**

Dix, Beulah Marie. Across the border; a play of the present, in one act and four scenes. New York: Henry Holt & Co., 1915. 3 p.l., 3–96 p., 2 pl. 12°.   **NBM**

—— Allison's lad, and other martial interludes. Being six one-act dramas, set forth by B. M. Dix. New York: Henry Holt and Co., 1910. 4 p.l., 3–214 p. 12°.   **NBM**

Allison's lad. The hundredth trick. The weakest link. The snare and the fowler. The captain of the gate. The dark of the dawn.

—— A legend of Saint Nicholas. (Poet lore. Boston, 1914. 8°. v. 25, p. 473–495.)   ***DA**

Dix, Beulah Marie, and EVELYN G. SUTHERLAND. A rose o' Plymouth-town. A romantic comedy in four acts. Boston: The Fortune Press, 1903. 5 p.l., 111 p., 1 l., 2 pl., 2 port. 8°.   **NBM**

Doctor Cure-All. [A comedy in two acts.] n. p. [189–?] 21 p. 12°.   **NBL p.v.11, no.5**

Title-page missing.

Doddridge, Joseph. Logan. The last of the race of Shikellemus chief of the Cayuga nation. A dramatic piece. To which is added. The dialogue of the backwoodsman, and the dandy, first recited at the Buffaloe Seminary, July the 1st, 1821. Buffaloe Creek, Brooke County, Va.: printed for the author, by Solomon Sala, 1823. 46 p., 1 l. 12°. **Reserve**

—— —— Reprinted: Cincinnati: Robert Clarke & Co., 1868. 2 p.l., (1)4–76 p. 8°. **HBC**

Donoho, T. Seaton. Oliver Cromwell: a tragedy in five acts. Washington: W. H. Moore, 1860. 72 p. 16°. **NBL p.v.22, no.2**

Downing, Henry Francis. The shuttlecock; or, Israel in Russia; an original drama in four acts. London: F. Griffiths [1913]. 96 p. 12°. **NBL p.v.32, no.4**

Doyle, Edward. Cagliostro. A dramatic poem in five acts. New York: printed for the author by W. B. Smith & Co. [cop. 1882.] 131 p. 12°. **NBM**

—— The comet: a play of our times. [In verse.] Boston: R. G. Badger, 1908. 176 p. 12°. **NBM**

Doyle, Edwin Adams. Phocion. A dramatic poem, and other poems. Winchester, Ohio: the author, 1910. vii, 214 p., 1 pl. 12°. **NBI**

Phocion, p. 3–72.

Dramatic pieces, calculated to exemplify the mode of conduct which will render young ladies both amiable and happy, when their school education is completed. New-Haven: printed by Abel Morse, 1791. 3 v. in 1. 12°. **Reserve**

v. 1. The good mother-in-law. The good daughter-in-law.
v. 2. The reformation. The maternal sister.
v. 3. The triumph of reason. The contrast.

Dreiser, Theodore. The blue sphere; a drama. (Smart set. New York, 1914. 8°. v. 44, p. 245–252.) **NBA**

Drey, Sylvan. Woman's rights; a comedy. Baltimore: Cushings & Bailey, 1884. 45 p. 12°. **NBL p.v.18, no.21**

Drogheda, pseud. of A. S. Moore? Cosmos. [A play in three acts, and in verse.] Nashville, Tenn.: Cumberland Presbyterian Publishing House, 1885. 136 p. 8°. **NBM**

The **Drunkard;** or, The fallen saved! A moral domestic drama in five acts. Boston: Jones's Publishing House, 1847. 1 p.l., (1)6–50 p. 12°. (Boston Museum edition of American acting dramas. no. 1.) **NBL p.v.9, no.8**

Duganne, Augustine Joseph Hickey. Woman's vows and Mason's oaths; a play in four acts. To which are added, a description of the costumes...and the whole of the stage business. New York: R. M. De Witt. cop. 1874. 76 p. 12°. (De Witt's acting plays. no. 161.) **NBL p.v.30, no.4**

Dumas, William Charles. Belshazzar. [Drama in five acts.] Boston: R. G. Badger [1912]. 120 p. 12°. ***PSQ**

Dumont, Frank. The cake walk. A farce in one scene. Chicago: The Dramatic Publishing Company [cop. 1897]. 1 p.l., 5–8 p. 12°. (The darkey & comic drama.) **NBL p.v.14, no.6**

—— Conrad; or, The hand of a friend. Drama in three acts. Chicago: The Dramatic Pub. Co. [cop. 1897.] 39 p. 12°. (Sergel's acting drama. no. 508.) **NBL p.v.4, no.16**

—— Gambrinus, king of lager beer. A diabolical, musical, comical and nonsensical Ethiopian burlesque. Music arranged for the pianoforte by A. B. Sedgwick. New York: The Dramatic Publishing Company, cop. 1876. 19 p. 12°. (De Witt's Ethiopian and comic drama. no. 106.) **NBL p.v.5, no.1**

—— Get-Rich-Quick Society; or, One hundred for thirty. Farce. Chicago: The Dramatic Publishing Company, cop. 1898. 7 p. 12°. (The darkey & comic drama.) **NBL p.v.14, no.5**

—— A girl of the century. A comedy in one act. Philadelphia: Penn Publishing Co., 1897. 13 p. 12°. **NBL p.v.11, no.2**

—— The girl from Klondike; or, Wideawake Nell. A comedy-drama, in three acts. Chicago: The Dramatic Publishing Company, cop. 1898. 26 p. 12°. (American acting drama.) **NBL p.v.18, no.2**

—— Scenes in front of a clothing store. A farce, in one scene. New York: The Dramatic Publishing Company, cop. 1889. 6 p. 12°. (De Witt's Ethiopian and comic drama. no. 160.) **NBL p.v.21, no.6**

—— The yellow kid who lives in Hogan's alley. A burlesque. New York: The Dramatic Publishing Company, cop. 1897. 9 p. 12°. (De Witt's Ethiopian and comic drama. no. 164.) **NBL p.v.18, no.1**

Duncan, Florence I. Ye last sweet thing in corners. Being ye faithful drama of ye artists' vendetta. By F. I. D. Philadelphia: Duncan & Hall [cop. 1880]. 66 p. 12°. **NBM**

Dunlap, William. Abaellino, the great bandit. A grand dramatic romance, in five acts. [By J. H. D. Zschokke.] Translated from the German, and adapted to the New-York theatre, by William Dunlap. New-York: D. Longworth, 1807. 63 p. 2. ed. 24°. **NCO p.v.291**

—— —— New-York: T. Longworth, 1820. 66 p. 4. ed. 16°. **NGB p.v.157, no.6**

—— The Africans; or, War, love, and duty. A play, in three acts. [By William Dunlap.] Philadelphia: M. Carey, 1811. 1 p.l., (1)88–169 p. 16°. **NBM p.v.9**

—— André: a tragedy, in five acts: as performed by the Old American Company, New York, March 30, 1798. To which are added, authentic documents respecting Major André: consisting of letters to Miss Seward, the Cow chace, proceedings of the court martial. &c... New-York: Printed by T. & J. Swords, 1798. viii, (1)10–109 p., 1 l. 8°. **Reserve**

—— André: a tragedy, in five acts [and in verse]: as now performing at the theatre in New York. [By William Dunlap.] To which is added, the Cowchace: a satirical poem. By Major André: with the proceedings of the court-martial; and authentic documents concerning him. London: Printed for David Ogilvy and son, 1799. viii, (1)10–110 p., 1 l. 8°. **Reserve**

—— André; a tragedy in five acts, with an introduction by Brander Matthews. [To which are added authentic documents respecting Major André; consisting of letters to Miss Seward, the Cow Chace, proceedings of the court martial, etc.] New York: The Dunlap Society, 1887. xxxiii p., 1 l., 139 p., 1 port. 8°. (Dunlap Society. Publications. v. 4.) **NBL (Dunlap)**
This edition, limited to one hundred and seventy-five copies, is a reprint from the 1798 edition of J. & T. Swords of New York.

—— The archers, or Mountaineers of Switzerland; an opera, in three acts, as performed by the Old American Company, in New-York; to which is subjoined a brief historical account of Switzerland ... [By William Dunlap.] New-York: Printed by T. & J. Swords, 1796. viii, (1) 10–94 p., 1 l. 8°. **Reserve**

—— Darby's return, an interlude... New-York: David Longworth, 1807. 3 p.l., (1)218–225 p. 16°. **NBM p.v.8**

—— Darby's return. A comic sketch. As performed at the New York Theatre November 24th, 1789, for the benefit of Mr. Wignell. New York: Hodge, Allen & Campbell, 1789. [Facsimile reprint, 1899.] 14 p., 1 l. 8°. (Appendix to P. L. Ford, Washington and the theatre. New York, 1899. 8°. Dunlap Society. Publications. new series, no. 8.) **NBL (Dunlap)**

—— The dramatic works of William Dunlap. In ten volumes. v. 1–2. Philadelphia and New York, 1806–16. 16°. **Reserve**
v. 1 has imprint: Philadelphia: T. & G. Palmer, 1806; v. 2 has imprint: New-York: D. Longworth, 1816.
v. 1. The father of an only child. Leicester. Fontainville Abbey. Darby's return.
v. 2. Voice of nature. Fraternal discord. Italian father. Good neighbor.

—— The father; or, American Shandyism. A comedy, as performed at the New-York Theatre, by the Old American Com-

pany. Written in the Year 1788. [By William Dunlap.] New-York: Printed by Hodge, Allen & Campbell, 1789. 3 p.l., (1)6–56 p., 1 l. 8°. **Reserve**
First published in the Massachusetts magazine: or, Monthly Museum, v. 1, Oct. – Nov., 1789, p. 620–629, 649–655.

—— With an introduction by Thomas J. McKee. New York: The Dunlap Society, 1887. xii p., 2 l., (1)4–68 p., 1 pl. 8°. (Dunlap Society. Publications. no. 2.) **NBL (Dunlap)**
This edition was limited to one hundred and seventy-five copies.

—— Fraternal discord: a drama, in five acts. Altered from the German of A. Von Kotzebue... New York: D. Longworth, 1809. 69 p. 16°. **NBM p.v.8**

—— The glory of Columbia, her yeomanry! A play, in five acts. New York: David Longworth, 1817. 56 p. 16°. **NBM p.v.8**

—— The good neighbor: an interlude, in one act. New-York: David Longworth, 1814. 12 p. 16°. **NBM p.v.8**

—— The Italian father: a comedy, in five acts. New-York: D. Longworth, 1810. 63 p. 16°. **NBM p.v.8**

—— Leicester, a tragedy... New-York: David Longworth, 1807. 2 p.l., (1) 90–150 p. 16°. **NBM**

—— Lovers vows; a play, in five acts. From the German of Kotzebue. New-York: David Longworth, 1814. 74 p. 16°. **NBM p.v.8**

—— Peter the Great; or, The Russian mother: a play. In five acts. New-York: David Longworth, 1814. 56 p. 16°. **NBM p.v.8**

—— Ribbemont; or, The feudal baron, a tragedy in five acts. New York: D. Longworth, 1803. 72 p. 16°. **NBM**

—— Rinaldo Rinaldini; or, The great banditti. A tragedy in five acts. By an American and a citizen of New York [i. e., William Dunlap]. New York: the author, 1810. v(i), (1)8–82 p., 1 pl. 24°. **NCO p.v.292, no.4**

—— Tell truth and shame the devil: a comedy, in two acts, as performed by the Old American Company, New-York, January, 1797. [By William Dunlap.] New-York: Printed by T. and J. Swords, 1797. 3 p.l., (1)6–45(1) p. 8°. **Reserve**

—— The virgin of the sun: a play, in five acts. From the German of Augustus von Kotzebue. With notes marking the variations from the original. [By William Dunlap.] New-York: printed by G. F. Hopkins, for William Dunlap, 1800. iv p., 1 l., (1)8–80 p. 8°. (German theatre. no. 2.) **Reserve**
Prompter's copy, interleaved. With ms. notes.

—— The voice of nature: a drama, in three acts. Translated and altered from a

French melo drame, called The judgment of Solomon... New York: David Longworth, 1807. 41(1) p., 1 l. 2. ed. 16°.
NBM p.v.8

—— The wife of two husbands: a drama, in five acts... New-York: D. Longworth, 1811. 55 p. 2. ed. 16°. **NBM p.v.8**

—— The wild-goose chace: a play, in four acts. With songs. From the German of Augustus von Kotzebue. With notes marking the variations from the original. [Also. The life of Kotzebue, written by himself.] New-York: Printed by G. F. Hopkins, for William Dunlap, and sold at the office of the printer [and others], 1800. x p., 1 l., (1)10–104 p., 2 fronts. 8°. (German theatre. no. 1.)
Reserve

—— Yankee chronology; or, Huzza for the Constitution! A musical interlude, in one act. To which are added, the patriotic songs of The freedom of the seas, and Yankee tars. New-York: D. Longworth, 1812. 16 p. 16°. **NBM p.v.8**

A **Dutchman** in Ireland. A comic sketch. Chicago: The Dramatic Publishing Company [18—?]. 8 p. 12°. (The darkey & comic drama.) **NBL p.v.14, no.4**

E., A. Matchmakers. A comedy in one act. Boston: W. H. Baker & Co. [cop. 1884.] 30 p. 12°. (Baker's edition of plays.) **NBL p.v.18, no.9**

Ebin, Alex. B. "Marriageables." A farcical comedy from modern life in New York — in three acts. [New York,] cop. 1912. 64 p. 8°. **NBL p.v.29, no.7**

—— "Portia in politics." A play in three acts. [New York,] cop. 1912. 64 p. 8°.
NBL p.v.29, no.8

Eddy, Marion. The outcast's daughter. A drama in four acts. Chicago: The Dramatic Pub. Co. [cop. 1899.] 32 p. 12°. (Sergel's acting drama.) **NBL p.v.4, no.15**

Eggerth, Werner. My own philosophy, and other poems and dramas. Chicago: The Lakeside Press, R. R. Donnelley & Sons Company [cop. 1909]. x, 292 p., 1 l. 8°. **NBI**
The dramas are: Among the pioneers. Strife and peace. The last of the Barotins.

Ehrmann, Max. Jesus: a passion play. New York: Baker & Taylor Co. [cop. 1915.] 282 p. 12°. **NBM**

Eliot, Annie. The green-room rivals. A comedietta in one act. Boston: W. H. Baker & Co., 1894. 16 p. 12°. (Baker's edition of plays.) **NBL p.v.19, no.1**

Ellet, Elizabeth Fries Lummis. Teresa Contarini: a tragedy, in five acts. (In her: Poems, translated and original. Philadelphia, 1835. 16°. p. 137–229.) **NBHD**

Elliott, William. Fiesco: a tragedy. By an American [i. e., William Elliott]. New York: published for the author, 1850. iv p., 1 l., 7–64 p. 12°. **NBM p.v.1**

Elliston, A. Louis. An unlucky tip. A comedietta in one act. Boston: W. H. Baker & Co., 1903. 29 p. 12°. (Baker's edition of plays.) **NBL p.v.19, no.16**

Emerson, William R. Putkins. Heir to — Castles in the air. A comic drama, in one act... Boston: G. M. Baker & Co. [cop. 1871.] 16 p. 12°.
NBL p.v.5, no.6

Emmons, R. Tecumseh; or, The battle of the Thames, a national drama, in five acts. Philadelphia, 1836. 36 p. 12°.
NBM p.v.3

Enander, Hilma L. Three plays. Boston: R. G. Badger [1913]. 75 p. 12°. **NBM**
In the light of the stone. The man who did not understand. On the trail.

English, Thomas Dunn. The Mormons; or, Life at Salt Lake City. A drama, in three acts...as performed at Burton's Theatre, March, 1858. New York: S. French [1858]. 43 p. 12°. (French's standard drama, acting edition. no. 205.)
ZZMG p.v.21, no.5

Eno, Henry Lane. The Baglioni. A play in five acts. New York: Moffat, Yard & Co., 1905. 4 p.l., 148 p. 8°. **NBM**

Eshobel, Raymond. How much I loved thee! A drama. [Washington, D. C.: the author, cop. 1884.] vi p., 1 l., 153 p. 12°.
NBM

Eustaphieve, Alexis. Alexis, the czarewitz. A tragedy in five acts. (In his: Reflections, notes, and original anecdotes, illustrating the character of Peter the Great. Boston, 1814. 2. ed. 12°. p. 141–224.) **GLF**

Evans, Florence Wilkinson. The ride home. Poems: with The marriage of Guineth, a play in one act. Boston: Houghton Mifflin Co., 1913. xi(i), 388 p., 1 l. 12°. **NBI**

Evans, Nathaniel. An Exercise; containing, A Dialogue and Ode on Occasion of the Peace. Performed at the Public Commencement in the College of Philadelphia, May 17th, 1763. (In his: Poems on several occasions. Philadelphia, 1772. 8°. p. 72–81.) **Reserve**

The **Eve** of St. John. A melodramatic spectacle in three acts. Version of Naiad queen. [18—?] 2 p.l., 24 l. f°. **† NCOF**
Manuscript promptbook.

Everett, David. Daranzel; or, The Persian patriot. An original drama. In five acts. [In verse.] Boston: John Russell, 1800. 66 p., 1 l. 8°. **NBL p.v.13, no.3**

Ewer, William Brooks. Prince Charming; a play in a prologue and three acts.

[In verse.] Middletown, N. Y.: Hanford & Horton Co.. 1913. 48 p.. 1 port. 2. ed. 8°.   NBL p.v.29, no.1

Ewing, Thomas, the younger. Jonathan; a tragedy. [In five acts and in verse.] New York: Funk & Wagnalls Co., 1902. 148 p. 12°.   *PSQ

Fairman, James. The voice of the sea. A comedy, in three acts. n. p.: the author [cop. 1882]. 103 p. 8°.   NBL p.v.13, no.5

Faugéres, Margaretta Bleecker. Belisarius: a tragedy. New York: Printed by T. and J Swords, 1795. 53 p. 8°. Reserve

Fawcett, Edgar. The Buntling ball; a Græco-American play, being a poetical satire on New York society. Illustrations by C. D. Weldon. New York: Funk & Wagnalls, 1884. 154 p. illus. 8°.   NBM
Published anonymously.

—— —— New York: Funk & Wagnalls, 1885. 154 p. illus. 8°.   NBM

—— The new King Arthur: an opera without music. New York: Funk & Wagnalls, 1885. iv p., 1 l., (1)8–164 p. 12°.   NBM

—— —— New York: Funk & Wagnalls, 1885. iv p., 1 l., (1)8–164 p. 2. ed. 12°.   NBM

Federalism triumphant in the steady habits of Connecticut alone, or, The turnpike road to a fortune. A comic opera, or, political farce in six acts, as performed at the Theatres Royal and Aristocratic at Hartford and New-Haven October 1801. n. p.: printed in the year 1802. 40 p. 8°.   IQL

Felix, F. Pontia: the daughter of Pilate. Drama in four acts. Baltimore: J. Murphy Co., 1899. 52 p. 12°.   NBL p.v.18, no.15

—— The shepherdess of Lourdes; or, The blind princess. A drama in five acts. Baltimore: John Murphy Co., 1899. 66 p. 12°.   NBL p.v.19, no.15

Fernald, Chester Bailey. The cat and the cherub; a play in one act. New York: S. French. 1912. 35 p. illus. 12°. (French's acting edition of plays. v. 162, no. 3.)   NCO

—— The married woman; a play in three acts. London: Sidgwick & Jackson, Ltd., 1913. 111(1) p. 12°.   NBM

—— The pursuit of Pamela; a comedy. [In 4 acts.] New York: S. French, 1914. viii, 96 p., 4 pl. 12°. (French's acting edition. no. 2527.)   NCO p.v.386, no.1

Ficke, Arthur Davison. Mr. Faust. [A play in 5 acts and in verse.] New York: Mitchell Kennerley. 1913. ix(i), 115 p. 12°. (Modern drama series.)   NBM

Field, Henrietta Dexter, and R. M. Field. The muses up to date. [Short plays for children.] Chicago: Way & Williams, 1897. xi p., 1 l., 11–278 p., 1 l. 12°. NAS
The muses up to date. Cinderella. Trouble in the garden. The modern Cinderella. The wooing of Penelope. A lesson from fairy land.

Field, Kate. Extremes meet. A comedietta... London: Samuel French [18—?]. 16 p. 12°.   NCO p.v.266

Fields, Annie Adams. Orpheus: a masque. Boston: Houghton, Mifflin & Co., 1900. 3 p.l., 42 p., 1 pl. 8°.   NBM

Fillmore, J. E. War. A play in one act. (Poet lore. Boston, 1914. 8°. v. 25, p. 523–533.)   *DA

Finch, Lucine. The butterfly. (Poet lore. Boston, 1910. 8°. v. 21, p. 401–414.)   *DA

Fiske, Isabella Howe. A comedy of the exile. (Poet lore. Boston, 1906. 8°. v. 17, no. 1, March, 1906, p. 51–58.)   *DA

Fitch, Clyde. Barbara Frietchie, the Frederick girl. A play in four acts. New York City: Life Pub. Co., 1900. 128 p., 10 pl., 2 port. 8°.   NBM

—— Beau Brummel. A play in four acts written for Richard Mansfield. New York: John Lane Co., 1908. 142 p., 8 pl., 1 port. 8°.   NBM

—— Captain Jinks of the horse marines. A fantastic comedy in three acts. New York: Doubleday, Page & Co., 1902. 6 p.l., 3–166 p., 1 l., 15 pl., 1 port. 8°.   NBM

—— The climbers. A play in four acts. New York: The Macmillan Co., 1906. 265 p. 12°.   NBM

—— The girl with the green eyes. A play in four acts. New York: The Macmillan Co., 1905. 200 p. 12°.   NBM

—— Her own way. A play in four acts. New York: The Macmillan Co., 1907. xiii, 235 p. 12°.   NBM

—— Nathan Hale. A play in four acts. New York: R. H. Russell, 1899. 6 p.l., 100 p., 12 pl. 8°.   NBM

—— The stubbornness of Geraldine. A play in four acts. New York: The Macmillan Co., 1906. xi, 214 p. 12°.   NBM

—— The truth. A play in four acts. New York: The Macmillan Co., 1907. xiii, 237 p. 12°.   NBM
Also printed in T. H. Dickinson's Chief contemporary dramatists, p. 237–282.

Fitzpatrick, Ernest Hugh. Magdalene of France; an historical drama in four acts. Pontiac, Ill.: The Sentinel Pub. Co., 1907. 62 p., 12 pl., 2 port. 8°.
                                   NBL p.v.12, no.16

Fitzpatrick, F. W. The fall of Babylon. The scenario of a spectacular drama. Washington, D. C.: Shaw Bros., 1910. 18 p. illus. 8°.   NBL p.v.13, no.12

Flora; or, The lover's ordeal. An operetta in two acts. Huntington: Long-Islander Print, 1857. 7 l. 16°.
NBL p.v.17, no.5

Follen, Eliza Lee Cabot, compiler. Home dramas for young people. Boston and Cambridge: James Munroe and Company, 1859. vi p., 2 l., (1)4–441 p. 12°.
NBM

For love. A drama in three acts. [18—?] 3 pamphlets. 4°.   **†NCOF**
Prompter's manuscript copy.

Ford, Alfred. Scenes and sonnets. New York: Tappen Bowne, printer [cop. 1872]. 31 p. 12°.   **NBH p.v.33, no.7**
The plays included are: Jael and Sisera: a woman's rights drama and The five hour law: or, Scenes in Athens.

Ford, Paul Leicester. "The best laid plans." As enacted in Two social cups of tea, Two social jokes, and One social agony. [By P. L. Ford.] [New York?] 1889. 27 p. 8°.   **NBL p.v.10, no.13**

Forrest, Thomas. The disappointment; or, The force of credulity. A new comic-opera, in three acts. By Andrew Barton [pseud.]. Second Edition, revised and corrected, with large additions by the Author. Philadelphia: printed for and sold by Francis Shallus, 1796. iv p., 1 l., (1)8–94 p., 1 l. 12°.   **Reserve**

The Forty thieves; a grand melodramatic romance, in two acts. New York: S. French [18—?]. 26 p. 12°. (French's American drama. no. 21.)   **NBM p.v.2**

Foulke, William Dudley. Maya; a drama. [In five acts and in verse.] New York: Cosmopolitan Press, 1911. 70 p. 12°.   **NBM**

Fowler, Manly B. The prophecy; or, Love and friendship: a drama in three acts. New York: Murden & Thomson, 1821. 34 p. 16°.   **NCO p.v.251, no.10**

Frank, Florence Kiper. Jael; a poetic drama in one act. Chicago: The Little Theatre, 1914. 29(1) p. 12°.   ***PSQ**

Frank, Maude Morrison. Short plays about famous authors. New York: Henry Holt and Company, 1915. vii, 144 p. 12°.
NBM

A mistake at the manor. When Heine was twenty-one. Miss Burney at Court. A Christmas eve with Charles Dickens. The fairies' plea.

Frank Glynn's wife; or, An American harem. A comedietta in one act. Chicago: The Dramatic Publishing Company [cop. 1897]. 14 p. 12°. (Sergel's acting drama. no. 461.)   **NBL p.v.2, no.1**

Franklin, Frank Milton. Prince and profligate: a drama in four acts. New York: S. French [cop. 1904]. 4 p.l., 145 p. 8°.   **NBM**

Franklin, S. A question of honor. A dramatic sketch in one act. Philadelphia: Penn Pub. Co., 1899. 19 p. 12°. (Dramatic library. v. 1, no. 188.)
NBL p.v.19, no.10

Fraser, John A. Because I love you. Drama in four acts. Chicago: The Dramatic Publishing Company [cop. 1899]. 60 p. 12°. (Sergel's acting drama. no. 447.)
NBL p.v.2, no.3

—— Bloomer girls; or, Courtship in the twentieth century. A satirical comedy in one act. Chicago: The Dramatic Pub. Co. [cop. 1896.] 23 p. 12°. (American amateur drama.)   **NBL p.v.6, no.4**

—— A cheerful liar. Farcical comedy in three acts. Chicago: The Dramatic Publishing Company [cop. 1896]. 56 p. 12°. (Sergel's acting drama. no. 415.)
NBL p.v.2, no.2

—— A delicate question. An original comedy drama in four acts. Author's edition. Chicago: The Dramatic Publishing Company [cop. 1896]. 64 p. 12°. (American amateur drama.)
NBL p.v. 18, no.5

—— A modern Ananias. A comedy in three acts. Author's edition. Chicago: The Dramatic Publishing Company [cop. 1895]. 66 p. 12°. (Sergel's acting drama. no. 361.)   **NBL p.v.2, no.6**

—— Santiago; or, For the red, white and blue. A war drama in four acts. Chicago: The Dramatic Publishing Company [cop. 1898]. 58 p., 1 pl. 12°. (Sergel's acting drama. no. 314.)   **NBL p.v.2, no.5**

—— The showman's ward. A comedy in three acts. Chicago: The Dramatic Pub. Co. [cop. 1896.] 49 p. 12°. (American amateur drama.)   **NBL p.v.6, no.3**

—— 'Twixt love and money. A comedy drama in four acts. Chicago: The Dramatic Publishing Company [cop. 1896]. 68 p. 12°. (American acting drama.)
NBL p.v.18, no.4

—— A woman's honor. Drama in four acts. Chicago: The Dramatic Publishing Company [cop. 1899]. 53 p. 12°. (Sergel's acting drama. no. 431.)   **NBL p.v.2, no.4**

Freybe, C. E. In garrison. (Poet lore. Boston, 1915. 4°. v. 26, p. 499–511.) ***DA**

Fuller, Henry Blake. The puppet-booth. Twelve plays. New York: The Century Co., 1896. 4 p.l., 212 p. 12°.   **NBM**
The cure of souls. On the whirlwind. The love of love. Afterglow. The ship comes in. At Saint Judas's. The light that always is. The dead-and-alive. Northern lights. The story-spinner. The stranger within the gates. In such a night.

Fuller, Horace W. Dear uncle. A comedy in four acts. Adapted from the French of "L'Héritage de M. Plumet." New York: Dramatic Pub. Co., cop. 1890. 42 p. 12°. (De Witt's acting plays. no. 353.)   **NBL p.v.18, no.13**

Furman, A. A. Philip of Pokanoket; an Indian drama. New York: Stettner, Lambert and Co., 1894. 136 p. 12°.   **HBC**

Furniss, Grace Livingston. A box of monkeys. New York: Harper & Bros. ₁cop. 1891.₁ 2 p.l., (1)4–61 p. 16°.
NBL p.v.32, no.9

—— The corner lot chorus. A farce in one act. Boston: W. H. Baker & Co. ₁cop. 1891.₁ 19 p. 12°. (Baker's edition of plays.)   NBL p.v.19, no.6

—— The Jack trust. New York: Harper & Bros. ₁cop. 1891.₁ 2 p.l., (1)4–63 p. 16°.   NBL p.v.31, no.2

—— Tulu. New York: Harper & Bros. ₁cop. 1891.₁ 2 p.l., (1)4–87 p. 16°.
NBL p.v.31, no.3

—— The veneered savage. New York: Harper & Bros. ₁cop. 1891.₁ 2 p.l., (1)4–33 p. 16°.   NBL p.v.31, no.4

Gale, Jane Winsor. Victoria; a comedy in three short acts. (Poet lore. Boston, 1915. 8°. 26, p. 78–110.)   *DA

Gale, Zona. The neighbours. (In: T. H. Dickinson, editor, Wisconsin plays. New York, 1914. 12°. p. 1–67.)   NBL

Gardiner, Margaret Doane. Universal neurasthenia; or, The house of rest. New York: F. F. Sherman, 1909. 29 p. 8°.
NBM

Gardner, Nelson. Two dramas and one song. New York: Press of The Friedman Print, 1907. 73 l. 16°. NBL p.v.11, no.3
The plays are Clio and Lycaon and The martyred maid.

Garnett, Porter. The green knight; a vision. Music by E. G. Stricklen, with a cover design by A. Putnam; decorations by R. W. Hart & E. Neuhaus... The ninth grove play of the Bohemian Club of San Francisco, as...performed...on the occasion of the club's thirty-fourth annual midsummer jinks... San Francisco: privately printed for the Bohemian Club ₁by Taylor, Nash & Taylor,₁ 1911. xxviii, 62 p., 1 l., 1 plan, 1 pl. 8°.   NBM

Gates, Eleanor. "We are seven"; a three-act whimsical farce. New York: Arrow Pub. Co. ₁1915.₁ 166 p. 8°. NBM

Gayarré, Charles Étienne Arthur. The school for politics. A dramatic novel. New York: D. Appleton & Co., 1854. 158 p. 12°.   NBM

Gayler, Charles. The son of the night. A drama, in three days: and a prologue ... New York: S. French ₁1857₁. 42 p. 12°. (French's standard drama. no. 169.)
NBM p.v.2

—— —— Same.   NCOF
Prompter's copy, interleaved. With ms. notes.

Gentlemen coons' parade. Musical sketch, in one act. Chicago: The Dramatic Publishing Company, cop. 1885. 8 p. 12°. (The darkey & comic drama.)
NBL p.v.19, no.7

Getchell, W. P. A fisherman's luck. A comedy-drama in four acts. Boston: W. H. Baker & Co. ₁cop. 1893.₁ 47 p. 12°. (Baker's edition of plays.)
NBL p.v.19, no.3

Gibson, Preston. S. O. S.; a play in one act. Adapted, with permission of publisher, from a short story by Leonard Merrick. New York: S. French, 1912. 32 p. 12°.   NBL p.v.28, no.2

Gildehaus, Charles. Æneas. A drama. Saint Louis: A. Ungar & Co., prtrs., 1884. 54 p. 8°.   NBL p.v.24, no.8

—— Plays. Sibyl. Telemachus. Aeneas. ₁In verse.₁ Saint Louis: J. L. Boland Book and Stationery Co., 1888. iv p., 2 l., 258 p. 12°.   NBM

Gillette, William. Electricity; a comedy in three acts. (Drama. Chicago, 1913. 8°. 1913, no. 12, p. 12–123.)   NAFA

Gilmore, Marion Forster. Virginia: a tragedy, and other poems. Louisville, Kentucky: J. P. Morton & Co., 1910. 4 p.l., 79 p. 8°.   NBI

Godfrey, Thomas, the younger. Juvenile poems on various subjects. With The Prince of Parthia, a tragedy... To which is prefixed, Some Account of the Author and his Writings. Philadelphia, Printed by Henry Miller, 1765. xxvi p., 1 l., 223 p. 4°.   Reserve

Goldschmidt, William. Hadassah; or, The Persian queen. Operetta in three acts. Music by S. Sabel. n. p., cop. 1891. 35 p. 8°.   *PSQ

Goodloe, Abbie Carter. Antinoüs. A tragedy. Philadelphia: J. B. Lippincott Co., 1891. 139 p. 12°.   NBM

Goodman, Kenneth Sawyer. Back of the Yards. A play in one act. New York: D. C. Vaughan, 1914. 44 p. 12°. (Stage Guild plays.)   NBL p.v.32, no.3

—— Dust of the road; a play in one act. Chicago: Stage Guild ₁1912₁. 21 p. 8°.
NBL p.v.28, no.10

—— Ephraim and the winged bear; a Christmas-eve nightmare in one act. New York: D. C. Vaughan, 1914. 31(1) p. 12°.
NBL p.v.32, no.2

Goodman, Kenneth Sawyer, and T. W. STEVENS. A pageant for Independence day. Chicago: Stage Guild ₁cop. 1912₁. 20 l. illus. 8°.   NBL p.v.28, no.1

Gould, Edward Sherman. "The very age!" A comedy, in five acts. New York: D. Appleton & Co., 1850. 153 p. 12°.
NBM p.v.3

Grand-bas, and LOIN-OW, pseuds. Receipt for newly-married people. A comedy, in one act only, but quite a number of touching scenes. Prepared for the occasion by Grand-bas and Loin-ow. Albany: Weed, Parsons and Co., 1877. 42 p. 24°.   NBL p.v.31, no.6

Grant, Percy Stickney. The return of Odysseus; a poetic drama in four acts. New York: Brentano, 1912. 6 p.l., 5–132 p. 8°. **NBM**

Grant, Robert. The lambs. A tragedy. Illustrated. Boston: J. R. Osgood & Co., 1883. 61 p. 12°. **NBM**

The **Gray** tigers of Smithville; or, He would and he wouldn't: a school extravaganza in three acts, edited by E. Roth. Philadelphia, 1887. iv, 5–80 p. 16°. (American school and college plays. no. 1.) **NBL p.v.20, no.10**

Green, Anna Katherine, afterwards Mrs. Charles Rohlfs. Risifi's daughter. A drama. New York: G. P. Putnam's Sons, 1887. 2 p.l., 109 p. 12°. **NBM**

Greene, Clay M. The dispensation, and other plays. New York: G. H. Doran Co. [1914.] 4 p.l., 5–96 p. 12°. **NBM**
The dispensation. The star of Bethlehem. "Through Christmas bells." The awakening of Barbizon.

Greene, H. Copley. Théophile, a miracle play. Boston: Small, Maynard & Co., 1898. viii, 32 p., 1 pl. 12°. **NBM**

Greenough, J. B. Queen of hearts, a dramatic fantasia. Boston: Ginn, Heath & Co., 1885. 46 p. 12°. (Diversions for students. no. 1.) **MZB p.v.3, no.2**

—— The rose and the ring. Adapted for the private stage from Thackeray's Christmas pantomime. By the author of "The queen of hearts." Cambridge: C. W. Sever, 1880. 43 p. 12°. **NBL p.v.9, no.4**

Griffith, Helen Sherman. The burglar alarm. A comedietta in one act. Philadelphia: The Penn Pub. Co., 1899. 17 p. 12°. (Dramatic library. v. 1, no. 180.) **NBL p.v.18, no.6**

—— Help wanted: a comedy in two acts. Philadelphia: The Penn Pub. Co., 1908. 27 p. 12°. **NBL p.v.6, no.12**

Griffith, William. Trialogues. Kansas City, Mo.: Hudson-Kimberly Pub. Co., 1897. 2 p.l., ix-xii, 65 p. 12°. **NBM**
Spring. Summer. Autumn. Winter.

Groff, Alice. Freedom. A play in four acts. Boston: R. G. Badger, 1904. 58 p. 12°. **NBM**

Gross, Samuel Eberly. The merchant prince of Cornville. A comedy. Chicago: Rand, McNally & Company [cop. 1896]. 168 p. 8°. **NBM**

Gundelfinger, George Frederick. The ice lens; a four-act play on college morals (causes and consequences). New York: Shakespeare Press, 1913. 212 p. 12°. **NBM**

Guptill, Elizabeth F. A trip to storyland. A musical play for children. Chicago: T. S. Denison [cop. 1908]. 46 p. 12°. (Denison's specialties.) **NBL p.v.8, no.9**

Hagedorn, Hermann. The horse thieves. A comedy in one act. [Boston:] privately reprinted from the Boston Transcript, May, 1909. 45 p., 2 pl. 8°. **NBM**

—— Makers of madness; a play in one act and three scenes. New York: Macmillan Co., 1914. 95 p. 12°. **NBM**

—— The silver blade. A drama in one act. [In verse.] Berlin: A. Unger, 1907. 61 p. 8°. **NBM**

Hageman, Maurice. The first kiss. A comedy in one act. Chicago: The Dramatic Publishing Company [cop. 1897]. 16 p. 12°. (American acting drama.) **NBL p.v.19, no.9**

—— Hector. A farce in one act. Chicago: The Dramatic Publishing Company [cop. 1897]. 1 p.l., 5–23 p. 12°. **NBL p.v.19, no.13**

—— Professor Robinson. Comedy in one act. Chicago: The Dramatic Publishing Company [cop. 1899]. 18 p. 12°. (American acting drama.) **NBL p.v.17, no.2**

—— To rent. Comedietta in one act. Chicago: The Dramatic Publishing Co. [1898.] 10 p. 12°. (American acting drama.) **NBL p.v.4, no.19**

—— Two veterans. Farce in one act. Chicago: The Dramatic Publishing Company [cop. 1899]. 12 p. 12°. (American acting drama.) **NBL p.v.18, no.3**

—— What became of Parker. A farce comedy in four acts. Chicago: The Dramatic Publishing Company [cop. 1898]. 72 p. 8°. (Sergel's acting drama. no. 443.) **NBL p.v.2, no.3**

Haid, P. Leo. Major John André: an historical drama in five acts. Baltimore: J. Murphy & Co., 1876. vi p., 1 l., 9–68 p. 12°. **NBM p.v.1**

Hall, Louisa Jane Park. Miriam. A dramatic poem. Boston: H. P. Nichols & Co., 1838. viii p., 1 l., 122 p. 2. ed. 12°. **NBM p.v.3**

—— Miriam, and Joanna of Naples, with other pieces in verse and prose. Boston: Wm. Crosby and H. P. Nichols, 1850. 4 p.l., (1) 6–403 p. 12°. **NBY**
Miriam: a dramatic poem, p. 11–111.

Hamilton, Alexander, 1786–1875. Cromwell: a tragedy in five acts [and in verse] by the author of "Thomas a Becket" [i. e. Alexander Hamilton]. New York: Dick & Fitzgerald [cop. 1868]. 3 p.l., (1)6–124 p. 12°. **NBM**

—— Dramas and poems. New York: Dick & Fitzgerald [cop. 1887]. vii, 124, 106 p., 2 l., 9–133 p. 12°. **NBM**
The dramas are Cromwell, Thomas a' Becket and Canonicus.

—— Thomas a' Becket: a tragedy in five acts. New York: Dick & Fitzgerald [cop. 1863]. 106 p. 12°. **NBM**

Haney, John Louis. Monsieur D'Or; a dramatic fantasy. Philadelphia: The Egerton Press, 1910. 145 p. 12°. **NBM**

Hanna, Elizabeth Heming. The court of Juno. A lyrical drama in two acts. Atlanta, Ga.: ₍Franklin Print. & Pub. Co.,₎ 1903. 46 p. 16°.   **NBL p.v.22, no.12**

Hanshew, T. W. The 'forty-niners; a drama of the gold mines. (Reprinted in: Alfred Bates, editor, The drama. London, 1903. 8°. v. 20, p. 233–275.)   **NAF**

Hapgood, Neith Boyce. Winter's night; a play in one act. By Neith Boyce. (Trend. New York, 1914. 8°. v. 7, p. 524–530.)   ***DA**

Harby, Isaac. Alberti, a play, in five acts. (In his: A selection from the miscellaneous writings of the late Isaac Harby. Charleston, 1829. 8°. p. 3–54.)   **NBQ**

Harper, John Murdoch. Champlain; a drama in three acts. ₍In verse.₎ With an introduction entitled: Twenty years and after. Toronto: Trade Pub. Co. ₍cop. 1908.₎ 296 p., 1 pl. 8°.   **NCR**

Harrigan, Edward. The blue and the grey. A dramatic sketch, in two scenes. New York, 1875. 12 p. 12°.
          NBL p.v.32, no.11

Harrison, Constance Cary. Alice in Wonderland. A play for children in three acts: dramatized by Mrs. Harrison. Illustrations by J. Tenniel. Chicago: The Dramatic Publishing Company ₍cop. 1890₎. 35 p. 12°. (Children's plays.)
          NBL p.v.19, no.5

Harte, Bret. Two men of Sandy Bar. A drama ₍in four acts₎. Boston: Houghton, Mifflin & Co., 1882. 151 p. 16°. **NBM**

Hartmann, Karl Sadakichi. Buddha. A drama in twelve scenes. New York: author's edition, 1897. 45 p. 12°. **NBM**

—— Christ. A dramatic poem in three acts. ₍Boston:₎ author's edition, 1893. 81 p. 12°.   **NBM**

—— A tragedy in a New York flat. A dramatic episode in two scenes. New York: the author, 1896. 11 p. 8°.
          NBL p.v.10, no.6

Haviland, J. Butler. Miss Jones, journalist; or, For the special edition. A farcical sketch in one act. Boston: W. H. Baker & Co., 1904. 11 p. 12°. (Vaudeville stage.)   **NBL p.v.1, no.16**

—— Mrs. Maltby's mole; or, The copper casket. A farcical sketch in one act. Boston: W. H. Baker & Co., 1904. 11 p. 12°. (Vaudeville stage.) **NBL p.v.1, no.15**

Hayward, Edward F. The mothers. Boston: Richard G. Badger, 1903. 27 p. 16°.   **NBM**

Hazelton, George Cochrane, the younger, and J. H. BENRIMO. The yellow jacket; a Chinese play done in a Chinese manner. In three acts. Illustrated by A. Genthe. ₍Introduction by Brander Matthews.₎ Indianapolis: Bobbs-Merrill Co. ₍1913.₎ 8 p.l., 190 p., 11 pl. 12°.   **NBM**

Head, Edward Francis. Poltroonius. A tragic farce, in one act. By an admirer of chivalry ₍i. e. E. F. Head₎. Boston: A. Williams & Co., 1856. 31 p. 12°.
          NBX p.v.8, no.7
A satire on Brooks's assault of Senator Sumner.

Heath, J. E. Whigs and Democrats; or, Love of no politics. A comedy in three acts. Richmond: T. W. White, 1839. vi, (1)8–80 p. 8°.   ***C p.v.313, no.7**

Heavysege, Charles. Saul. A drama, in three parts. Boston: Fields, Osgood & Co., 1869. 436, 5 p. new ed. 16°. ***PSQ**

—— —— New York: Lovell Print. & Pub. Co., 1876. 436, 5 p. new ed. 12°.
          *PSQ

Heermans, Forbes. Down the Black Cañon; or, The silent witness. A drama of the Rocky Mountains. In four acts. Chicago: The Dramatic Publishing Company, cop. 1890. 40 p. 12°. (Sergel's acting drama. no. 357.) **NBL p.v.2, no.9**

Henderson, Daniel McIntyre, the younger. Santa Claus' dilemma. A whimsical musical Christmas comedy. ₍In verse.₎ New York: Dick & Fitzgerald, 1909. 14 p. 12°.   **NBL p.v.7**

Hentz, Caroline Lee Whiting. De Lara; or, The Moorish bride. A tragedy in five acts ₍1852?₎ 27 l. f°.   **†NCOF**
Manuscript promptbook.

Hepner, Adolf. Good night, Schatz! Realistic joke and earnest, in one act. St. Louis, Mo.: The St. Louis News Co., 1894. 47(1) p. 12°.   **NBL p.v.5, no.2**

H. M. S. "Parliament," or, The lady who loved a government clerk. Ottawa: Citizen Printing and Publishing Company. 1880. 37 p. 8°.   **HWD p.v.50**

The **Hero** of two wars, a drama in five acts. (Truth's advocate and monthly anti-Jackson expositor. Cincinnati, 1828. 8°. March, p. 111–112; April, p. 142–143; May, p. 182–183; June, p. 238–239; July, p. 266–267; Aug., p. 308–311; Oct., p. 389.) **II**
The Library lacks the issue for Sept., 1828. A political attack on Andrew Jackson. Signed W.

Heron, Matilda. Camille; or, The fate of a coquette. Adapted from the French of Alexandre Dumas, jr. ₍by Matilda Heron.₎ New York: S. French ₍185–?₎. 42 p. 12°. (French's American drama. The acting edition. no. 129.)   **NCOF**

—— —— Cincinnati: T. Wrightson & Co., 1856. 64 p. 8°. **NKM p.v.176, no.2**

Herts, Benjamin Russell. The female of the species. (International. New York, 1915. 4°. v. 9, p. 152–154.) ***DA**

Heywood, Joseph Converse. Antonius. A dramatic poem. New York: Hurd and Houghton, 1867. 272 p. 12°. **NBM**

——— Herodias. A dramatic poem. New York: Hurd & Houghton, 1867. 251 p. 12°. **NBM**

——— Salome. A dramatic poem. New York: Hurd & Houghton, 1867. 222 p. 12°. ***PSQ**

Higgins, Aileen Cleveland. Thekla. A drama. Boston: The Poet Lore Co., 1907. 62 p. 12°. **NBM**

Hiland, Frank E. The curtain lifted; or, The order of the sons of Mars. A burlesque initiation ceremony. Chicago: The Dramatic Publishing Co. [1896.] 20 p. 12°. **NBL p.v.4, no.18**

Hill, David. Bound by an oath. A domestic drama in four acts and a prologue. Boston: W. H. Baker & Co. [cop. 1890.] 80 p. 12°. (Baker's edition of plays.) **NBL p.v.18, no.8**

——— Joining the Tinpanites; or, Paddy McFling's experience. A mock initiation for the amusement and instruction of secret societies... (In three parts.) Boston: W. H. Baker & Co. [cop. 1891.] 3 pamphlets. 12°. (Baker's novelties.) **NBL p.v.18, no.10–12**

——— Out of his sphere. A drama in three acts. Boston: W. H. Baker & Co. [cop. 1889.] 35 p. 12°. (Baker's edition of plays.) **NBL p.v.19, no.8**

Hillhouse, James Abraham. Dramas, discourses, and other pieces. Boston: Charles C. Little and James Brown, 1839. 2 v. 12°. **NBM**

The dramas included are Demetria, Hadad, and Percy's masque.

——— Hadad, a dramatic poem. New York: E. Bliss & E. White, 1825. x p., 1 l., (1)14–208 p. 8°. ***PSQ**

Hilliard, Robert. The littlest girl. A play in one act. Dramatized by Robert Hilliard from R. H. Davis's story, "Her first appearance." Chicago: The Dramatic Publishing Company [cop. 1898]. 10 p. 12°. (American acting drama.) **NBL p.v.15, no.7**

Hinckley, Henry Barrett. Poems. Northampton, Mass.: The Nonotuck Press, 1909. 39 p. 8°. **NBL p.v.11, no.15**

Caesar's wife, p. 5–26. Oberon and Titania, p. 31–35.

Hobart, George Vere. Experience: a morality play of today. Acting version. New York: The H. K. Fly Company [cop. 1915]. 128 p., 11 pl. 12°. **NBM**

Hobart, Marie Elizabeth Jefferys. Athanasius; a mystery play, in three acts and a prologue. London: Longmans, Green, and Co., 1911. vii, 121 p., 7 pl. 8°. (Saint Agnes' mystery plays.) **NBM**

Hobbes, John Oliver, pseud. *See* **Craigie**, Pearl Mary Teresa Richards.

Hodgkinson, John. The man of fortitude; or, The knight's adventure. A drama in three acts. New York: D. Longworth, 1807. 32 p. 16°. **NBM p.v.7**

Hollenius, Laurence John. Dollars and cents. An original American comedy, in three acts. New York: Robert M. De Witt, cop. 1867. 40 p. 2. ed. 12°. **NBL p.v.19, no.2**

Hollister, Gideon Hiram. Thomas à Becket: a tragedy, and other poems. Boston: W. V. Spencer, 1866. iv p., 1 l., 186 p., 3 l. 12°. **NBM**

Hooker, Brian. Fairyland. An opera in three acts. New Haven: Yale University Press, 1915. 137 p. 8°. **NBM**

——— Mona; an opera in three acts. The poem by Brian Hooker; the music by Horatio Parker. New York: Dodd, Mead and Company, 1911. ix p., 1 l., 190 p. 12°. **NBM**

Hopkinson, Francis. An exercise; Containing a Dialogue and Ode, on the accession of his present gracious majesty George III. — Performed at a public commencement in the College of Philadelphia, May, 1762. (In his: The miscellaneous essays and occasional writings of Francis Hopkinson. Philadelphia, 1792. 8°. v. 3. [Part 2], Poems, p. 83–91.) **Reserve**

Hopp, Julius. Tears. A drama of modern life in four acts. Boston: The Poet-Lore Co., 1904. 78 p. 12°. **NBM**

Hotchkiss, G. B. The birthright: a romantic comedy of old France. Naugatuck [Conn.]: The Perry Press, 1906. 56 p. 8°. (Yale University prize poem, 1906.) **STG**

Hovey, Richard. The birth of Galahad. [A romantic drama.] Boston: Small, Maynard & Co., 1898. 2 p.l., 124 p. 12°. (In his: Launcelot and Guenevere: a poem in dramas. v. 3.) **NBM**

——— New York: Duffield & Co., 1907. 2 p.l., 124 p. 16°. (In his: Launcelot and Guenevere: a poem in dramas. v. 3.) **NBM**

——— The Holy Graal, and other fragments by Richard Hovey, being the uncompleted parts of the Arthurian dramas. Edited with introduction and notes by Mrs. Richard Hovey and a preface by Bliss Carman. New York: Duffield & Company, 1907. 128 p. 16° **NBM**

The Holy Graal. Astolat. Fata Morgana. King Arthur. Avalon.

——— The marriage of Guenevere. [A tragedy.] Boston: Small, Maynard & Co., 1898. 179 p. 12°. (In his: Launcelot and Guenevere: a poem in dramas. v. 2.) **NBM**

—— —— New York: Duffield & Co., 1907. 3 p.l., 171 p. 16°. (In his: Launcelot and Guenevere: a poem in dramas. v. 2.)   NBM

—— The quest of Merlin. ₍A masque.₎ Boston: Small, Maynard & Co., 1898. 2 p.l., 80 p. 12°. (In his: Launcelot and Guenevere: a poem in dramas. v. 1.) NBM

—— —— New York: Duffield & Co., 1907. 3 p.l., 3–80 p. 12°. (In his: Launcelot and Guenevere: a poem in dramas. v. 1.)   NBM

—— Taliesin. A masque. Boston: Small, Maynard & Co., 1900. 2 p.l., 58 p. 16°. (In his: Launcelot and Guenevere: a poem in dramas. v. 4.)   NBM

—— —— New York: Duffield & Co., 1907. 2 p.l., 58 p. 16°. (In his: Launcelot and Guenevere: a poem in dramas. v. 4.)   NBM

Howard, Bronson. The Henrietta; a comedy in four acts. London: S. French, Ltd., cop. 1901. 82 p. 12°. (French's acting edition of plays. v. 157.)   NCO

—— —— New York: S. French, 1901. 82 p. 8°.   NBL p.v.12, no.7

—— Kate. A comedy in four acts. New York: Harper & Bros., 1906. x, 210 p., 1 l. 12°.   NBM

—— Old love-letters. A comedy in one act. London: S. French, Ltd., cop. 1897. 24 p. 12°. (French's acting edition of plays. v. 142 ₍no. 2₎.)   NCO

—— ₍18—?₎ 2 p.l., 22 f. 4°.   † NCOF
Prompter's manuscript copy.

—— Shenandoah: a military comedy in four acts. New York: S. French ₍cop. 1897₎. 71 p. 8°.   NBL p.v.12, no.8

—— Young Mrs. Winthrop. A play in four acts. New York: Madison Square Theatre, 1882. 47 p. 8°. NBL p.v.11, no.13

—— —— Same.   NCOF
Prompter's copy, interleaved. With ms. notes.

Howard, Homer Hildreth. The child in the house. A play in one act. (Poet lore. Boston, 1913. 8°. v. 24, p. 433–444.) *DA

Howard, Katharine. Candle flame; a play ₍for reading only₎. Boston: Sherman, French & Co., 1914. 6 p.l., 32 p. 8°.   NBI

Howe, J. B. The woman of the world; or, A peep at the vices and virtues of country and city life. An entirely original drama in four acts. New York: Happy Hours Co. ₍1858?₎ 36 p. 12°. (The acting drama. no. 100.)   NCO p.v.301, no.9

Howe, Julia Ward. The world's own. Boston: Ticknor and Fields, 1857. 141 p. 12°.   NBM

Howell, S. A marriage for revenge. A drama in five acts. New Orleans: Office of the Picayune, 1874. 34 p. 12°.
NBL p.v.1, no.3

Howell-Carter, Josephine. Hilarion. A one-act play. (Poet lore. Boston, 1915. 8°. v. 26, p. 374–392.)   *DA

Howells, William Dean. The Albany depot. ₍A farce.₎ New York: Harper & Bros., 1892. 68 p. 24°. (Harper's black and white series.)   NBM

—— —— New York: Harper & Bros., 1893. 68 p. 24°. (Harper's black and white series.)   NBM

—— Bride roses; a scene. Boston: Houghton, Mifflin and Co., 1900. 48 p., 1 l. 16°.   NBM

—— A counterfeit presentment. Comedy. Boston: Houghton, Mifflin & Co., 1880. 199 p. 16°.   NBM

—— The elevator; a farce. ₍In three acts.₎ Boston: Houghton, Mifflin & Co. ₍cop. 1885.₎ 84 p. 16°.   NBM

—— Evening dress: a farce. New York: Harper & Brothers, 1893. 2 p.l., 159 p., 3 pl. 24°. (Harper's black and white series.)   NBM

—— The garroters. Farce... New York: Harper and Bros., 1894. 90 p., 4 pl. 24°. (Harper's black and white series.)   NBM

—— An Indian giver; a comedy. ₍In one act.₎ Boston: Houghton, Mifflin and Co., 1900. 99(1) p. 16°.   NBM

—— A letter of introduction: a farce. New York: Harper & Brothers ₍cop. 1892₎. 61 p., 4 pl. 24°. (Harper's black and white series.)   NBM

—— The mother and the father. Dramatic passages. New York: Harper & Brothers, 1909. 4 p.l., 3–54 p., 1 l., 4 pl. 8°.   NBI

—— The mouse-trap, and other farces. New York: Harper & Brothers ₍cop. 1889₎. 5 p.l., (1)4–184 p. 12°.   NBM
The garroters. Five o'clock tea. The mouse-trap. A likely story.

—— Out of the question; a comedy. ₍In six acts.₎ Boston: Houghton, Mifflin & Co. ₍1905.₎ 3 p.l., (1)6–183 p. 16°. NBM

—— The parlor car; a farce. ₍In one act.₎ Boston: Houghton, Mifflin & Co. ₍cop. 1904.₎ 74 p., 1 l. 16°.   NBM

—— A previous engagement. Comedy. New York: Harper & Brothers, 1897. 3 p.l., 65 p., 3 pl. 16°.   NBM

—— The register; a farce. ₍In one act.₎ Boston: Houghton, Mifflin and Co. ₍cop. 1884.₎ 91 p. 16°.   NBM

—— Room forty-five; a farce. ₍In one act.₎ Boston: Houghton, Mifflin and Co., 1900. 61(1) p. 16°.   NBM

—— A sea-change; or, Love's stowaway. A lyricated farce, in two acts and an epilogue. Boston: Ticknor and Co., 1888. 151 p. 16°.   NBM

—— The sleeping car; a farce. [In one act.] Boston: Houghton Mifflin Co., 1912. 2 p.l., (1)4–74 p. 16°. **NBM**

—— The smoking car; a farce. [In one act.] Boston: Houghton, Mifflin and Co., 1900. 70 p., 1 l. 16°. **NBM**

—— The unexpected guests; a farce. New York: Harper & Brothers, 1893. 2 p.l., 54 p., 7 pl. 24°. (Harper's black and white series.) **NBM**

Howie, H. M. After the matinee. A comedy in one act. Philadelphia: The Penn Pub. Co., 1899. 19 p. 12°. (Dramatic library. v. 1, no. 185.) **NBL p.v.18, no.14**

—— The reformer reformed. A comedy sketch. Philadelphia: Penn Pub. Co., 1899. 11 p. 12°. (Dramatic library. v. 1, no. 187.) **NBL p.v.18, no.7**

Hoyt, Charles H., and EDWARD SOLOMON. Lyrics of the maid and the moonshiner. Written by Chas. H. Hoyt; composed by Edward Solomon. First produced at the Standard Theatre, New York, August 16, 1886, under the management of Mr. Jas. C. Duff. New York: P. F. McBreen [1886]. 1 p.l., 24 p. 12°. **NBL p.v.21, no.8**

Hubbell, Horatio. Arnold; or, The treason of West Point. A tragedy in five acts. Philadelphia: [H. Young,] 1847. 76 p. 12°. **NBL p.v.19, no.11**

Hubner, Charles William. Cinderella; or, The silver slipper. Lyrical drama in four acts. Atlanta, Georgia: Dodson & Scott, 1879. 24 p. 8°. **NBL p.v.10, no.8**

—— The maid of San-Domingo. A drama in three acts. (In his: Wild flowers. New York, 1877. 12°. p. 5–73.) **NBI**

Hughes, Elizabeth. Women for votes. [Drama in three acts.] New York: E. P. Dutton & Co., 1912. 2 p.l., 97 p. 12°. **NBM**

Humphreys, David. The widow of Malabar; or, The tyranny of custom: a tragedy. Imitated from the French of M. Le Mierre. (In his: The miscellaneous works of Colonel Humphreys. New-York, 1790. 8°. p. 115–176.) **NBG**

Huntington, Gurdon. The shadowy land, and other poems, (including The guests of Brazil). New York: James Miller, 1861. 1 p.l., (1)6–506 p., 1 l. 8°. **NBI**
The guests of Brazil; or, The martyrdom of Frederick: a tragedy, p. 409–506.

Hutchins, Will. Jeanne d'Arc at Vaucouleurs. (A romantic drama for the stage.) (Poet lore. Boston, 1910. 8°. v. 21, p. 97–148.) ***DA**

Hutton, Joseph. Fashionable follies: a comedy, in five acts... Philadelphia: James Lakin, 1815. ix p., 1 l., (1)14–76 p. 16°. **NBM p.v.5, no.1**

—— The orphan of Prague: a drama. in five acts. New-York: D. Longworth, 1810. 58 p. 16°. **NBM p.v.5, no.2**

—— The school for prodigals: a comedy, in five acts. New-York: D. Longworth, 1809. 62 p. 16°. **NBM p.v.5, no.4**

—— The wounded hussar, or The rightful heir: a musical afterpiece. In two acts, as performed at the New Theatre, Philadelphia. Philadelphia: Thomas T. Stiles, 1809. 24 p. 16°. **NBM p.v.5, no.3**

Iliowizi, Henry. Herod: a tragedy. Minneapolis, Minn.: [Tribune Book Rooms,] 1884. 80 p. 8°. ***PSQ**

—— Joseph: a dramatic representation in seven tableaux. Minneapolis, Minn.: The Tribune Job Printing Co., 1885. 46 p. 8°. **NBL p.v.24, no.6**

Irwin, Grace Luce. A close call. A farce in one act. Boston: W. H. Baker & Co., 1902. 24 p. 12°. (Baker's edition of plays.) **NBL p.v.16, no.22**

—— Drawing room plays. San Francisco: Paul Elder & Co., 1903. 3 p.l., 165 p. 12°. **NBM**
A domestic dilemma. Heroes. An innocent villain. Art for art's sake. An intimate acquaintance. The wedding of Mah Foy. Music hath charms.

—— A spoiled darling. A comedy in three acts. Boston: W. H. Baker & Co., 1903. 41 p. 12°. (Baker's edition of plays.) **NBL p.v.16, no.21**

Jacobson, Janie. Belshazzar; a Scriptural play in four acts. [New York: Schoen and Kellerman, 1911.] 11(1) p. 8°. ***PSQ**

—— For liberty. A Chanucah play in four acts. n. t.-p. [New York: Stettiner Bros.,] cop. 1905. 16 p. 8°. ***PSQ**

—— Joseph and his brethren. A Scriptural play in four acts. n. t.-p. [New York: Stettiner Bros., cop. 1905. 16 p. 8°. ***PSQ**

—— A maid of Persia. A Purim play in four acts. [New York,] 1905. 14 p. 8°. ***PSQ**

—— Ruth, the Moabitess; a Scriptural play in three acts. Jephthah's vow; a Scriptural play in two acts. [New York: Schoen & Kellerman, 1910.] 16 p. 8°. **NBL p.v.13, no.9**

James, Henry. Theatricals. Two comedies: Tenants, Disengaged. London: Osgood, McIlvaine & Co., 1894. vi p., 2 l., (1)4–325 p. 12°. **NBM**

Jaquith, Mrs. M. H. The "deestrick-skule" of fifty years ago. Chicago: The Dramatic Publishing Company, cop. 1888. 37 p. 12°. **NBL p.v.26, no.5**

—— "Exerbition" of the deestrick skule of fifty years ago. Chicago: Dramatic Publishing Company, cop. 1890. 50 p. 8°.
NBL p.v.24, no.7

Sequel to *The Deestrick-skule.*

—— Ma Dusenberry and her gearls. Humorous entertainment. First and second singin' "towers." Chicago: The Dramatic Publishing Company [cop. 1896]. 12 p. 12°.   NBL p.v.16, no.11

—— Parson Poor's donation party. Burlesque entertainment in two scenes. Chicago: The Dramatic Publishing Company [cop. 1896]. 1 p.l., 31–49 p. 12°. (Sergel's acting drama. no. 441.)
NBL p.v. 2, no.10

Jasper, Walter. Susanna. A drama in five acts [in blank verse]. Boston: Mayhew Pub. Co., 1908. 2 p.l., 100 p. 12°.
NBM

Jenkins, Floyd, and R. P. DARROW. The wilderness; an American play. New York: Broadway Pub. Co., 1912. 1 p.l., lxxii, 95 p. 12°.   NBM

Johnson, Daniel. Den politiska komedian i Europa... Öfversättning af Fredrik Sterky. Stockholm: A. V. Carlson, 1880. 213 p. 12°.   NIR p.v.32

Johnson, E. The mouth of gold: a series of dramatic sketches illustrating the life and times of Chrysostom. New York: A. S. Barnes & Co., 1873. 97 p. 16°. NBM

Johnson, Samuel D. The fireman: a drama in three acts... Boston: W. V. Spencer [pref. 1856]. 36 p. 12°. (Spencer's Boston theatre. no. 51.)   NCOF

Prompter's copy. With ms. notes.

Johnston, Mary. The goddess of reason. [A drama in five acts.] Boston: Houghton, Mifflin & Co., 1907. viii, 234 p., 1 l. 8°.   NBM

Jones, George. Tecumseh and the prophet of the West. An original historical Israel-Indian tragedy, in five acts... The life and history of General Harrison ... London: Longman, Brown, Green, and Longmans, 1844. 11 p.l., 196 p. 2. ed. 8°.   HBC

Jones, Joseph Stevens. Captain Kyd: or, The wizard of the sea... A drama... Boston: W. V. Spencer [18—?]. 44 p. nar. 8°. (Spencer's Boston theatre. no. 61.)
NCOF

Prompter's copy, interleaved. With ms. notes.

—— —— New York: S. French [18—?] 44 p. 12° (French's standard drama. The acting edition. no. 268.)   NCOF

Prompter's copy, interleaved. With ms. notes.

—— The carpenter of Rouen. A drama in four parts. [18—?] 4 pamphlets. f°.
† NCOF

Prompter's manuscript copy. The list of dramatis personae gives the cast of March 15, 1847, with the name of J. B. Wright as prompter.

—— The carpenter of Rouen; or, The massacre of St. Bartholomew: a romantic drama in four acts... London: T. H. Lacy [18—?]. 33 p. 12°.   NCOF

Prompter's copy, interleaved. With ms. notes.

—— The carpenter of Rouen; or, A revenge for the massacre of St. Bartholomew. A romantic drama in three acts. London: T. H. Lacy [18—?]. 39 p. 12°. (Lacy's acting edition of plays. v. 4.)
NCO

—— Moll Pitcher; or, The fortune teller of Lynn. A drama... Boston: W. V. Spencer, 1855. 64 p. 12°. (Spencer's Boston theatre. new series, no. 1.) NCOF

Prompter's copy, interleaved. With the stage directions underscored.

—— Solon Shingle; or, The people's lawyer. A comedy in two acts. Boston: W. H. Baker & Co., cop. 1890. 32 p. 12°. (Baker's edition of plays.)
NBL p.v.21, no.3

Reprinted in Alfred Bates, *The drama,* v. 20, p. 197–232.

—— —— Chicago: The Dramatic Publishing Company [18—?]. 24 p. 12°. (The world acting drama.)   NBL p.v.16, no.19

—— The usurper; or, Americans in Tripoli. A drama altered and compressed into three acts by J. Jones. Boston, 1842. 3 pamphlets. 8°.   † NCOF

Prompter's manuscript copy. On the title-page is written "J. B. Wright, prompter, Boston, 1842."

Jordan, Elizabeth Garver. The lady from Oklahoma; a comedy in four acts. New York: Harper & Brothers, 1911. 5 p.l., 3–255(1) p. 8°.   NBM

Joseph and his brethren. The Hebrew son; or, The child of Babylon. In three acts. New York, 1860. 3 pamphlets. f°.
† NCOF

Prompter's manuscript copy. With the parts of the different characters on loose sheets.

Josselyn, Robert. The coquette: a domestic drama in five acts. Austin [Texas]: the author, 1878. 54 p. 12°.
NBL p.v.6, no.19

Judah, Samuel Benjamin Herbert. The rose of Arragon; or, The vigil of St. Mark. A melo-drama, in two acts. New York: S. King, 1822. 38 p. 16°. NBM p.v.6, no.1

Judd, Sylvester, 1813–53. Philo: an evangeliad. Boston: Phillips, Sampson, and Co., 1850. 244 p. 12°.   NBM

Kaenders, P. The Easter fire on the hill of Slane. A drama in three acts. St. Louis, Mo.: B. Herder, 1906. 39 p. 12°.
NBL p.v.12, no.12

—— Lorna Doone: a romantic drama in four acts. (Adapted from Blackmore's story.) St. Louis, Mo.: B. Herder, 1906. 39 p. 12°.   NBL p.v.12, no.11

—— Lucius Flavus: a drama in five acts. (Adapted from Father Spillmann's story.) St. Louis, Mo.: B. Herder, 1908. 70 p. 12°. **NBL p.v.9, no.12**

—— The prince of Fez. A drama in three acts. St. Louis: B. Herder, 1906. 42 p. 2. ed. 12°. **NBL p.v.12, no.13**

Kane, Helen P. The best laid plans. A farce in one act. Philadelphia: Penn Pub. Co., 1904. 18 p. 12°. **NBL p.v.1, no.4**

—— A bundle of matches. A society comedy in two acts. New York: Dick & Fitzgerald, 1909. 28 p. 12°. **NBL p.v.7**

—— Under sailing orders; a comedy in one act. New York: Dick & Fitzgerald, 1912. 16 p. 12°. **NBL p.v.27, no.9**

—— The white dove of Oneida. A romantic drama in two acts and after-scene. New York: Dick & Fitzgerald, 1907. 18 p. 12°. **NBL p.v.7, no.19**

Kasper, Robert Adam. The man you love; a play in four acts. Boston: R. G. Badger [1914]. 148 p. 12°. (American dramatists series.) **NBM**

—— Some people marry; a play in three acts. Boston: R. G. Badger [1914]. 122 p. 12°. (American dramatists series.) **NBM**

Kastelic, G. A. Thirty hours for three thousand years; or, Heresy and planets. Comedy-drama in five acts. New York [1892]. 1 p.l., 47 p., 1 pl. 8°. **NBH p.v.52, no.7**

Kavanaugh, Katharine. A converted suffragist; a play in one act for female characters. New York: Dick & Fitzgerald, 1912. 8 p. 12°. **NBL p.v.27, no.5**

—— A gentle touch; vaudeville sketch in one act. New York: Dick & Fitzgerald, 1912. 10 p. 12°. **NBL p.v.27, no.3**

—— A stormy night; a comedy in one act. New York: Dick & Fitzgerald, 1912. 12 p. 12°. **NBL p.v.27, no.2**

Keim, De Benneville Randolph. Frederick the Great; or, Love and majesty. An historical drama of the life and times of a royal friend. In five acts... [Washington? cop. 1904.] 28 p., 6 pl., 1 port. 4°. **NBL p.v.25, no.12**

—— La Fayette, the man of two worlds ('L'homme des deux mondes'). An epic drama of the French alliance in five acts. [Washington? cop. 1902.] 27 p., 7 pl. 4°. **† NBM**

—— "Monmouth"; or, The treason of Charles Lee... A dramatic monograph of the American revolution. In one act... n. p.. 1907. 62–78 p., 1 pl. 4°. **† NBM**

Kellogg, Elizabeth. Merry Xmas! A farce in two scenes. Written once upon a time for the College Club. Cincinnati: U. P. James, 1910. 22 p. 12°. **NBL p.v.12, no.5**

Kemble, Frances Anne, afterwards Mrs. Pierce Butler. Plays. An English tragedy: a play, in five acts. Mary Stuart. Translated from the German of Schiller. Mademoiselle de Belle Isle. Translated from the French of Alexandre Dumas. London: Longman, Green, Longman, Roberts & Green, 1863. 5 p.l., 7–582 p. 12°. **NCOF**

Prompter's copy, partly interleaved, and with ms. notes.

—— The star of Seville, a drama in five acts. New York: Saunders & Otley, 1837. 3 p.l., 130 p. 12°. **NCO p.v.328, no.3**

Kemp, Harry. Judas. [A drama.] New York: Mitchell Kennerley, 1913. 3 p.l., 5–254 p. 12°. ***PSQ**

Kennedy, Charles Rann. The idol-breaker; a play of the present day, in five acts, scene individable, setting forth the story of a morning in the ripening summer. New York: Harper & Bros., 1914. 177(1) p., 1 port. 8°. **NCR**

—— The necessary evil; a one-act stage play for four persons: to be played in the light. New York: Harper & Bros., 1913. 110 p., 1 l. 8°. **NCR**

—— The servant in the house. [Drama in five acts.] Illustrated with portraits of the characters in the play. New York: Harper & Bros., 1908. 151(1) p., 1 pl., 7 port. 8°. **NCR**

—— The terrible meek; a one-act stage play for three voices: to be played in darkness. New York: Harper & Brothers, 1912. 4 p.l., 43(1) p., 1 port. 8°. **NCR**

—— The winterfeast. [A drama.] New York: Harper & Bros., 1908. 7 p.l., 13–159 p., 8 pl. 8°. **NCR**

Kennedy, Charles William, and J. S. WILSON. Pausanias. A dramatic poem. New York and Washington: The Neale Publishing Company, 1907. 60 p. 12°. **NBM**

Kenyon, Charles. Kindling; a comedy drama in three acts. With an introduction by Clayton Hamilton. Garden City: Doubleday, Page & Co., 1914. xxi(i), 147(1) p., 1 l., 1 pl., 1 port. 12°. (Drama League series of plays. v. 1.) **NBM**

Kenyon, Frances S. Up to Freddie. A farce in two acts...designed for girls' schools. Boston: W. H. Baker & Co., 1903. 33 p. 12°. (Baker's edition of plays.) **NBL p.v.16, no.18**

Kidder, Jerome. The drama of earth. New York: Adolphus Ranney, 1857. 360 p., 1 pl. 12°. **NBM**

King, Georgiana Goddard. The way of perfect love. New-York: Macmillan Co., 1908. viii, 108 p. 12°. **NBM**

Kiralfy, I. I. Kiralfy's grand historical spectacle America in four acts, and seven-

teen scenes... Music by A. Venanzi. ₁Chicago:₁ I. Kiralfy, 1893. 36 p., 6 pl. 8°.
MWE p.v.1, no.14

Kleene, Alice Cole. Kirstin; a play in four acts. ₁A version of the story of H. C. Andersen. In verse.₁ Boston: Sherman, French & Co., 1913. 4 p.l., 93 p. 12°.
NBM

Koopman, Harry Lyman. Orestes: a dramatic sketch, and other poems. Buffalo, N. Y.: Moulton, Wenborne & Co., 1888. 5 p.l., (1)10–192 p. 16°.   **NBI**

Lamb, Osborn Rennie. The Iberian. Anglo-Greek play. With music by H. C. Dixon. ₁New York: The Ames & Rollinson Press, cop. 1903.₁ 119 p. 12°.   **NBM**
no. 320 of 500 copies printed.

—— A sailor's sweetheart: a comedy in one act. New York: The Ames & Rollinson Press ₁1909₁. 67 p. 12°.   **NBM**

Landes, Leonard. The playwright: a comedy... ₁With His partner's wife: a play.₁ New York: Chambers Press ₁1900₁. 3 p.l., 91 p., 2 l., 55 p., 1 port. 8°.   **NBM**

Langner, Lawrence. Wedded: a social comedy ₁in one act₁. (Little review. Chicago, 1914. 8°. v. 1, no. 8, p. 8–18.)   ***DA**

"The Larks," pseud. The Shakespeare water-cure: a burlesque comedy in three acts. New York: H. Roorbach, cop. 1897. 42 p. 12°.   ***NDD p.v.1, no.11**

The **Last** of the Mohicans. An Indian drama in 4 acts. ₁From the novel of the same name by James Fenimore Cooper.₁ ₁1849?₁ 1 p.l., 107 f. 16°.   **NCOF**
Manuscript promptbook.

Latour, Eugene. Adorable Elizabeth. A comedy in one act. New York: The Roxbury Pub. Co. ₁cop. 1899.₁ 25 p. 16°. (The wizard series.)   **NBL p.v.11, no.6**

Lavelle, Alice Elizabeth. Puppets of fate; a drama in four acts and a prologue. Boston: Gorham Press ₁1914₁. 63 p. 12°. (American dramatists series. v. 2.) **NBM**

Lawrence, F. N. Lanty's luck; or, Falsely accused. A drama of Irish life in three acts. Boston: W. H. Baker & Co. ₁cop. 1897.₁ 30 p. 12°. (Baker's edition of plays.)   **NBL p.v.16, no.14**

Lawson, James. Dramatic sketch. Julian and Elphina. (In his: Tales and sketches, by a cosmopolite. New-York, 1830. 12°. p. 93–100.)   **NBO**

—— Giordano. A tragedy. New York: E. B. Clayton — G. & C. & H. Carvill, 1832. vi p., 1 l., (1)10–102 p., 1 l. 8°. **NBM**

—— —— Yonkers: printed, not published, 1867. 98 p. 4°.   **NBM**

—— —— Yonkers, 1875. 2 p.l., 107–192 p. 8°.   **NBM (Lawson), p.v.1**

—— Liddesdale; or, The border chief. A tragedy. ₁New York: printed, not published, Tinson, printer, 1861.₁ 114 p. 8°.
NBM

—— —— Yonkers, 1874. 101 p. 8°.
NBM (Lawson), p.v.1

—— The maiden's oath. A domestic tragedy. Yonkers, 1877. 2 p.l., 195–312 p. 8°.   **NBM (Lawson), p.v.1**

Lays of leisure. The Italian husband, a dramatic poem. The young dreamer, and fugitive offerings in verse. Philadelphia: printed by Jesper Harding, 1825. 2 p.l., ₁iii₁–iv p., 2 l., (1)12–107(1) p. 24°. **NBHD**
The Italian husband, p. 11–65.

Lazarus, Emma. The poems of Emma Lazarus. Boston: Houghton, Mifflin and Company, 1895. 2 v. 12°.   **NBI**
The Spagnoletto: a play in five acts, v. 1, p. 222–342; The dance to death; a historical tragedy in five acts, v. 2, p. 69–173.

—— Songs of a Semite: The dance to death, and other poems. New York: Office of "The American Hebrew," 1882. 4 p.l., (1)6–80 p. 8°.   **NBI**
The dance to death; a historical tragedy in five acts occupies p. 5–48.

Leacock, John. The fall of British tyranny; or, American liberty triumphant. The first campaign. A tragi-comedy of five acts, as lately planned at the Royal Theatrum Pandemonium at St. James. The principal place of action in America. Published according to Act of Parliament... Philadelphia: printed by Styner & Cist, 1776. 21–66 p. 8°.   **Reserve**
Imperfect copy, lacking all before p. 21; title taken from Sabin.

Leavitt, John McDowell. Afranius, and The Idumean, tragedies, with The Roman martyrs, and other poems. New York ₁Riverside, Cambridge, printed by H. O. Houghton & Co.₁, 1869. iv, 255 p. **NBM**

—— The siege of Babylon; a tragedy. New York: Hurd and Houghton, 1869. 47 p. 16°.   **NBL p.v.22, no.5**

Le Brandt, Joseph. The girl from Porto Rico. A farce comedy in three acts. New York: Dick & Fitzgerald, 1906. 66 p. 12°.
NBL p.v.7, no.1

Ledoux, Louis Vernon. Yzdra. A tragedy in three acts. New York: G. P. Putnam's Sons, 1909. vii, 174 p. 12°.
NBM

Lee, Agnes. The sharing. Boston: Sherman, French & Co., 1914. 4 p.l., 64 p. 12°.   **NBI**
The sharing; drama in 1 act and in verse. The silent house; drama in 1 act and in verse.

Leibson, Jacob J. Too much Haman. A Purim comedy. New York: Bloch Pub. Co. ₁1905.₁ 13 p. 8°.   ***PSQ**

Leighton, William, the younger. At the court of King Edwin. A drama. Philadelphia: J. B. Lippincott & Co., 1878. 2 p.l., 7–157 p. 12°. **NBM**

—— The sons of Godwin. A tragedy. Philadelphia: J. B. Lippincott & Co., 1877. 188 p. 12°. **NBM**

Lennox, Charlotte Ramsay. The sister: a comedy. London: J. Dodsley, 1769. 2 p.l., 75(1) p. 2. ed. 8°. **NCO p.v.102**

Leonard, William Ellery. Glory of the morning; a play in one act. Madison: Wisconsin Dramatic Society, 1912. 53(1) p. 12°. **NBL p.v.32, no.1**
Also printed in T. H. Dickinson's *Wisconsin plays.*

Lester, Francis. Flirtation cured. Farce comedy in one act. (Male characters.) New York: The Dramatic Publishing Company, cop. 1899. 1 p.l., 10 p. 16°. (The wizard series.) **NBL p.v.22, no.6**

—— The new squire. Comedy in one act (male characters). Chicago: The Dramatic Publishing Company, cop. 1899. 31 p. 12°. (Sergel's acting drama. no.557.) **NBL p.v.4, no.8**

Lévêque, Joseph Mark. Billy Bing, the bachelor from Birmingham. A curtain raiser, with a moral and three scenes. [New Orleans,] cop. 1908. 3 p.l., (1)6–41 p. 12°. **NBL p.v.13, no.6**

Levi Ben-Halpai, pseud. of E. A. Guy? The true history and tragedy of Joshua, the Messiah. Washington, D. C.: E. A. Guy, 1903. 1 p.l., 46 p. 8°. **ZFHH p.v.2, no.8**

Levy, Clifton Harby. Haman and Mordecai, a Purim-play, in five acts. Cincinnati: Bloch Pub. Co., 1886. 21 p. 12°. ***PSQ**

Levy, Leah. Bible plays for the Sabbath school. Abraham. New York: Bloch Pub. Co., 1901. 22 p. 16°. ***PSQ**

Lewis, Eliza Gabriella. The outlaw; a dramatic sketch. (In her: Poems. Brooklyn, 1850. 12°. p. 1–51.) **NBI**

Lewis, Estelle Anna Blanche Robinson. The king's stratagem; or, The pearl of Poland. A tragedy in five acts, by Stella [pseud.]. London: Trübner, 1874. 5 p.l., 94 p. 2. ed. 12°. **NBM**

—— Sappho; a tragedy in five acts, by Stella [pseud.]. London: Trübner & Co., 1875. vi p., 1 l., 132 p., 1 pl. 12°. **NBM**

—— —— London: Trübner & Co., 1876. xiv p., 1 l., 132 p., 1 pl., 1 port. 2. ed. 12°. **NBM**

—— —— London: Trübner & Co., 1878. xiv p., 1 l., 132 p., 1 pl., 1 port. 4. ed. 12°. **NBM**

—— —— London: Trübner & Co., 1881. xiv p., 1 l., 132 p., 1 pl., 1 port. 6. ed. 12°. **NBM**

Lindsey, William. Red wine of Roussillon; a play in four acts. Boston: Houghton Mifflin Co., 1915. 6 p.l., (1)+174 p., 1 l. 8°. **NBM**

Lindsley, A. B. Love and friendship; or, Yankee notions. A comedy in three acts. New York: D. Longworth, 1809. 58 p. 16°. **NBM p.v.5**

Lisanti, G. F. Little Harold; or, The suffragette. A play in four acts. New York: Nicoletti Bros. Press [1911]. 43 p. 12°. **NBL p.v.30, no.2**

Litchfield, Grace Denio. Collected poems. New York: G. P. Putnam's Sons, 1913. ix, 341 p. 12°. **NBM**
Vita: an allegorical drama, p. 33–87; The nun of Kent: a historical drama, p. 149–235.

—— Vita: a drama. Boston: R. G. Badger, 1904. 1 p.l., 56 p. 12°. **NBM**

Local hits; or, High life in New-Orleans. A comedy in one act. New Orleans: Office of the Orleanian, 1850. 52 p. 12°. **NBL p.v.16, no.10**

Locke, Belle Marshall. Breezy Point. A comedy in three acts... Boston: W. H. Baker & Co. [cop. 1898.] 50 p. 12°. (Baker's edition of plays.) **NBL p.v.16, no.12**

Lockwood, Ingersoll. Washington: a heroic drama of the Revolution, in five acts. New York: the author, 1875. 67 p. p. 12°. **NBM p.v.4**

Lodge, George Cabot. Cain. A drama. Boston: Houghton, Mifflin & Co., 1904. 6 p.l., 154 p., 1 l. 12°. **NBM**

—— Herakles. [Drama in verse.] Boston: Houghton Mifflin Co., 1908. v (i) p., 2 l., 3–271 (1) p., 1 l. 12°. **NBM**

Loevius, Frederick. A colony of cranks. A comedy in three acts. Time: present. Place: the United States of America. [New York: F. W. Heiss, 19—?] 34 p., 1 l. 12°. **NBL p.v.23, no.3**

—— A warrant. A play in five acts. By F. Thaumazo [pseud. of Frederick Loevius]. Brooklyn, N. Y., 1909. 64 p. 12°. **NBM**

Logan, Algernon Sydney. Messalina: a tragedy in five acts. Philadelphia: J. B. Lippincott Co., 1890. 147 p. 12°. **NBM**

—— Saul: a dramatic poem. Philadelphia: J. B. Lippincott & Co., 1883. 80 p. 12°. **NBM**

London, Jack. Scorn of women. In three acts. New York: Macmillan Co., 1906. x, 256 p. 12°. **NBM**

—— Theft; a play in four acts. New York: The Macmillan Company, 1910. xii p., 1 l., 272 p. 12°. **NBM**

Long, Lily Augusta. Radisson, the voyageur; a verse drama in four acts. New York: Henry Holt and Co., 1914. viii, 114 p., 1 l. 12°. **NBM**

Longfellow, Henry Wadsworth. Christus: a mystery. part 1. The divine tragedy. Boston: James R. Osgood and Company, 1872. iv p., 1 l., 159 p. 12°. **NBM**

—— The divine tragedy. Boston: James R. Osgood and Company, 1871. iv, 150 p. 12°. **NBM**

—— —— Boston: James R. Osgood and Company, 1871. iv p., 1 l., 313 p. 8°. **NBM**

—— The golden legend. Boston: Ticknor, Reed, and Fields, 1851. 2 p.l., 3–301 p. 12°. **NBI**

—— —— Boston: Ticknor, Reed, and Fields, 1853. 2 p.l., 3–301 p. 12°. **NBI**

—— The masque of Pandora, and other poems. Boston: James R. Osgood and Company, 1875. iv p., 1 l., (1)4–146 p. 12°. **NBI**

—— —— Boston: James R. Osgood and Company, 1876. 3 p.l., ₍iii-₎iv, (1)4–146 p. 12°. **NBM**

—— The New England tragedies. London: George Routledge and Sons, 1868. vi p., 1 l., 221(1) p., 1 l. 12°. **NBM**
Endicott. Giles Corey of the Salem Farms.

—— —— Authorized edition. Endicott. Giles Corey of the Salem Farms. Leipzig: Bernhard Tauchnitz, 1868. 4 p.l., (1)6–258 p., 1 l. 16°. (Collection of British authors. v. 982.) **NBM**

—— The Spanish student, and other poems. New York: John B. Alden, 1887. 2 p.l., (1)8–106 p. 12°. **NBI**
Bound with his: Voices of the night, Ballads, and other poems. New York, 1887. 12°.

Lord, Alice E. A vision's quest. A drama in five acts, representing the hopes and ambitions, the love, marriage, pleadings, discouragements, and achievements of Christopher Columbus, discoverer of America. Baltimore: Cushing & Company, 1899. 123 p., 1 pl. 12°. **NBM**

Lord, William Wilberforce. André; a tragedy in five acts. New York: C. Scribner, 1856. 138 p., 1 port. 8°. **NBM**

Lounsbery, Grace Constant. Delilah; a drama in three acts. New York: Scott-Thaw Co., 1904. 128 p. 16°. ***PSQ**

Low, Samuel. The politician out-witted, a comedy, in five acts. Written in the Year 1788. By an American ₍Samuel Low₎. New-York: Printed for the Author, by W. Ross, 1789. 71 p. 8°. **Reserve**

Lucas, Daniel Bedinger. Dramatic works of Daniel Bedinger Lucas. Edited by C. W. Kent and Virginia Lucas. With a critical introduction by C. F. T. Brooke. University of Virginia edition. Boston: R. G. Badger ₍1913₎. x p., 3 l., 9–271 p., 1 pl. 12°. **NBM**
The maid of Northumberland. Hildebrand. Kate McDonald.

—— The maid of Northumberland: a dramatic poem. New York: G. P. Putnam's Sons, 1879. 184 p. 12°. **NBM**

Luce, Grace A. Brass buttons. A comedy in three acts... Boston: W. H. Baker & Co., 1900. 37 p. 12°. (Baker's edition of plays.) **NBL p.v.16, no.16**

Ludington, Helen G. The suffragette; a comedy in one act for seven females. New York: S. French, cop. 1909. 2 p.l., (1)4–28 p. 12°. (French's acting edition of plays. v. 157.) **NCO**

Lydston, George Frank. The blood of the fathers, a play in four acts. Chicago: Riverton Press, 1912. 2 p.l., 7–241 p. 12°. **NBM**

McAvoy, Ballard Brownlee. Prince Richard. ₍Drama in five acts and in verse.₎ n. p., cop. 1902. 97 p. 16°. **NBM**

McBride, H. E. Striking oil. ₍Philadelphia: Penn Pub. Co., 1898.₎ 215–240 p. 12°. **NBL p.v.16, no.15**

McCabe, J. L. Maloney's wedding; an Irish farce comedy in three acts. Chicago, 1897. 1 p.l., 194 f. 4°. **NBM**
Typewritten.

McCarty, W. Page. The golden horseshoe. A drama. Richmond: F. A. Christian, 1876. 45 p. 8°. **NBL p.v.25, no.5**

McCord, Louisa Susannah Cheeves. Caius Gracchus. A tragedy, in five acts. New York: H. Kernot, 1851. 128 p. 12°. **NBM p.v.4**

McCracken, J. L. H. Earning a living. A comedy, in five acts. By a citizen of New York ₍i. e., J. L. H. McCracken₎. New York: Pudney & Russell, 1849. 63 p. 8°. **NBM**

Macdonald, M. Guatemozin. A drama. Philadelphia: J. B. Lippincott & Co., 1878. 191 p. 12°. **NBM**

McGee, Thomas D'Arcy. Sebastian; or, The Roman martyr; a drama ₍in four acts₎, founded on Cardinal Wiseman's celebrated tale of "Fabiola." New York: D. & J. Sadlier & Co., 1861. 52 p. 12°. **NBM**

Mackay, Constance D'Arcy. The festival of Pomona, a spring festival. (Drama. Chicago, 1915. 8°. 1915, p. 161–171.) **NAFA**

—— Patriotic plays and pageants for young people. New York: Henry Holt and Company, 1912. 2 p.l., iii–viii, 223 p. 8°. **NBM**

—— Plays of the pioneers. A book of historical pageant-plays... New York: Harper & Brothers, 1915. 5 p.l., 13–174 p., 1 l., 8 pl. 12°. **NBM**
The pioneers. The fountain of youth. Mayday. The vanishing race. The passing of Hiawatha. Dame Greel o' Portland town.

Mackaye, Mary Keith Medbery. Pride and prejudice. A play founded on Jane Austen's novel by Mrs. Steele Mackaye. New York: Duffield & Co., 1906. vii p., 3 l., 168 p., 1 pl. 8°. **NBM**

Mackaye, Percy. Anti-matrimony: a satirical comedy. New York: F. A. Stokes Co. [1910.] 7 p.l., 3–160 p., 1 pl. 12°. **NBM**

—— The Canterbury pilgrims, a comedy. New York: The Macmillan Co., 1903. 1 p.l., viii p., 1 l., 210 p., 1 fac. 12°. **NBM**

—— Fenris, the wolf. A tragedy [in four acts and in verse]. New York: Macmillan Company, 1905. 5 p.l., 150 p. 12°. **NBM**

—— A garland to Sylvia: a dramatic reverie. With a prologue. New-York: The Macmillan Co., 1910. xxiv, 177 p. 12°. **NBM**

—— Jeanne d'Arc. [A drama in five acts and in verse.] New York: Macmillan Co., 1907. ix p., 1 l., 163 p., 1 l., 3 pl. 12°. **NBM**

—— —— New York: Macmillan Co., 1911. viii p., 2 l., 163 p., 1 l., 3 pl. 12°. **NBM**

—— Mater: an American study in comedy. New York: The Macmillan Co., 1908. 6 p.l., 3–163 p. 8°. **NBM**

—— Saint Louis: a civic masque. Garden City: Doubleday, Page & Company, 1914. xxii, 99 p., 1 l., 1 pl. 12°. **NBM**

—— Sanctuary; a bird masque. [In verse.] With a prelude by Arvia Mackaye. Illustrated with photographs in color and monotone by Arnold Genthe. New York: F. A. Stokes Co. [1914.] xx, 71(1) p., 4 pl. illus. 12°. **NBM**
First published in the Century, v. 87, p. 547–557.

—— Sappho and Phaon. A tragedy set forth with a prologue, induction, prelude, interludes, and epilogue. New York: The Macmillan Co., 1907. xv(i) p., 1 l., 3–225 p. 12°. **NBM**

—— The scarecrow; or, The glass of truth. A tragedy of the ludicrous. New York: The Macmillan Co., 1908. xv, 179 p. 12°. **NBM**
Also printed in T. H. Dickinson's *Chief contemporary dramatists*, p. 357–393.

—— A thousand years ago; a romance of the Orient. [In four acts and in verse.] With an introduction by Clayton Hamilton. Garden City: Doubleday, Page & Co., 1914. xxiv, 130 p., 1 l. 12°. (Drama League series of plays. v. 2.) **NBM**

—— To-morrow; a play in three acts. New York: F. A. Stokes Company, 1912. ix, 176 p. 12°. **NBM**

—— Yankee fantasies; five one-act plays. New York: Duffield & Company. 1912. xiv p., 1 l., 169 p. 12°. **NBM**
Chuck: an orchard fantasy. Gettysburg: a woodshed commentary. The antick: a wayside sketch. The cat-boat: a fantasy for music. Sam Average: a silhouette.

McKinley, Henry J. Brigham Young; or, The prophet's last love. A play in three acts. San Francisco: Bacon & Co., 1870. 30 p. 12°. **ZZMG p.v.22, no.1**

McKnight, Levi Adolphus. Indiana; a drama of progress; a history of Indiana in a play of four acts. Fowler, Ind.: the author, 1908. 3 p.l., (1)10–50 p., 1 pl., 1 port. 8°. **NBL p.v.25, no.9**

MacMillan, Mary Louise. Short plays. Cincinnati: Stewart & Kidd, 1915. 4 p.l., 245 p. 2. ed. 12°. **NBM**
The shadowed star. The ring. The rose. Luck? Entr' acte. A woman's a woman for a' that. A fan and two candlesticks. A modern masque. The futurists. The gate of wishes.

MacPhail, Andrew. The land. A play of character in one act with five scenes, of which one scene only is here printed. (University magazine. Montreal, 1914. 8°. v. 13, p. 275–291.) **STK**

Maddox, D. S. The man from Arizona. A farce in one act. Philadelphia: Penn Pub. Co., 1899. 10 p. 12°. (Dramatic library. v. 1, no. 189.) **NBL p.v.17, no.10**

Madelaine, the belle of the Faubourg; a drama in three acts... Boston: W. V. Spencer, 1856. 40 p. 12°. (Spencer's Boston theatre. no. 49.) **NCOF**
Prompter's copy, interleaved. With ms. notes.

Mævonius, pseud. The plays of Mævonius: ex antiquitatis angiportibus. Praxiteles. Jamaica, Queensborough, N. Y.: The Marion Press, 1903. 56 p. 4°. **NBL p.v.25, no.11**
no. 72 of 300 copies printed.
A modern drama probably written by Thomas Dunkin Paret.

Magnus, Maurice. Eldyle. An æsthetic drama. New York: Ego Press, 1898. 28 p. 8°. **NBL p.v.24, no.11**
no. 49 of 250 copies printed.

Mair, Charles. Tecumseh: a drama ...and Canadian poems. Toronto: W. Briggs, 1901. 1 p.l., 276 p., 3 port. 2. ed. 12°. **NCM**

Malone, Walter. Claribel, and other poems. Louisville, Ky.: J. P. Morton & Co., 1882. 297 p. 12°. **NBI**
Inez: a tragedy, p. 7–82; Claribel: a tragedy, p. 143–231.

Mann, Arthur Sitgreaves. Prince Ivo of Bohemia. A romantic tragedy in five acts. [In verse.] New New: The Grafton Press [cop. 1906]. 84 p. 12°. **NBM**

Mann, Hugh. Bound & Free. Two dramas. Boston: R. G. Badger, 1905. 80 p. 12°. **NBM**

—— The New Lights. A drama... Boston: R. G. Badger, 1904. 51 p. 12°. **NBM**

Manners, J. Hartley. Happiness, and other plays. New York: Dodd, Mead & Co., 1914. 8 p.l., 5–170 p., 3 pl. 12°. **NBM**
Happiness, a study. Just as well, a twentieth-century romance. The day of dupes, an allegory.

Marble, Thomas Littlefield. The Hessian: a Revolutionary drama in three acts. Philadelphia: The Penn Publishing Co., 1908. 34 p. 12°.   **NBL p.v.6, no.11**

—— Mistress Penelope. A romantic drama in one act. Philadelphia: The Penn Pub. Co., 1907. 13 p. 12°. **NBL p.v.8, no.3**

—— The raiders. A military drama in three acts. Philadelphia: The Penn Pub. Co., 1907. 45 p. 12°.   **NBL p.v.8, no.4**

—— A royal runaway. A comedy in three acts. Philadelphia: The Penn Pub. Co., 1904. 35 p. 12°.   **NBL p.v.1, no.5**

Marchand, F. G. Un bonheur en attire un autre. Comédie en un acte et en vers. (Royal Society of Canada. Proceedings and transactions. Montreal, 1883. f°. v. 1, section 1, p. 139–165.)   *** EC**

—— Quelques scènes d'une comédie inédite. Les faux brillants. Comédie en cinq actes et en vers. (Royal Society of Canada. Proceedings and transactions. Montreal, 1883. f°. v. 1, section, 1, p. 21–38.)   *** EC**

Markoe, Peter. The patriot chief. A tragedy... Philadelphia: Printed for the Author, and sold by Wm. Prichard, 1784. 2 p.l. 70 p. 8°.   **Reserve**

Marsden, Frederick, pseud. See **Silver**, W. A.

Martin, William Frank. Sir Harry Vane: a drama in five acts. Boston: Roxburgh Pub. Co. [1907.] 263 p., 4 port. 8°.   **NBM**

Masters, Edgar Lee. The bread of idleness; a play in four acts. Chicago: The Rooks Press, 1911. 173 p. 12°.   **NBM**

—— The locket; a play in three acts. Chicago: The Rooks Press, 1910. 110 p. 12°.   **NBM**

—— Maximilian: a play in five acts. Boston: R. G. Badger, 1902. 154 p. 12°.   **NBM**

Mathews, Cornelius. Calmstorm, the reformer. A dramatic comment. New York: W. H. Tinson, 1853. 71 p. 16°.   **NBL p.v.14, no.1**

—— The politicians: a comedy, in five acts. New York, 1840. 118 p. 12°.   **NBM p.v.4**

—— Witchcraft: a tragedy, in five acts. New-York: S. French, 1852. 99 p. 24°.   **NBM**

The Library also has three prompter's copies, with ms. notes.

Mathews, Frances Aymar. The new professor. A comedy for ladies in one act. Chicago: The Dramatic Publishing Company [cop. 1903]. 15 p. 12°. (Sergel's acting drama. no. 530.) **NBL p.v.2, no.12**

Matthews, James Brander. "Edged tools." A play in four acts. New York: S. French, cop. 1873. 47 p. 12°. **NCOF**

Prompter's copy, interleaved. With ms. notes.

—— Too much Smith; or, Heredity. A physiological and psychological absurdity in one act. By Arthur Penn [pseud.]. [Adapted from the French play "La postérité d'un bourgmestre" by M. Uchard.] Boston: W. H. Baker & Co., 1902. 50 p., 1 l. 12°. (Baker's edition of plays.)   **NBL p.v.18, no.25**

May, Gordon V. The red rosette. A western drama in three acts. New York: Dick & Fitzgerald, 1907. 43 p. 12°.   **NBL p.v.7, no.2**

May, Noble. Late this morning; a monologue. New York: Dick & Fitzgerald, 1912. 7 p. 12°.   **NBL p.v.27, no.1**

Mead. Wall-street; or, Ten minutes before three. A farce, in three acts. New-York, 1819. 24 p. 16°.   **NBL p.v.15, no.1**
Imperfect, lacking all after p. 24.

Medina, Louisa H. Ernest Maltravers. [A drama in three acts.] London: John Dicks [18—?]. 18 p. 12°. (Dicks' standard plays. no. 379.)   **NCO p.v.301, no.7**

—— The last days of Pompeii. A dramatic spectacle, taken from Bulwer's celebrated novel of the same title. New York: S. French [18—?]. 31 p. 12°. (French's standard drama. no. 146.)   **NBM p.v.2**

—— Nick of the woods. A drama in three acts. Boston: S. V. Spencer [18—?]. 45 p. 12°.   **NCOF**
Prompter's copy, interleaved. With ms. notes.

—— —— New York: S. French [18—?] 30 p. 12°.   **NCOF**
Prompter's copy, interleaved. With ms. notes.

Mendes, Henry Pereira. Esther: a Purim play. New York: P. Cowen, 1899. 23 p. 16°.   *** PSQ**
Repr.: The American Hebrew.

—— Judas Maccabaeus. A Chanuka play for Sunday school children. New York: P. Cowen, 1898. 19 p. 16°. *** PSQ**

Merington, Marguerite. Cranford: a play. A comedy in three acts made from Mrs. Gaskell's famous story. New York: Fox, Duffield & Co., 1905. vi p., 1 l., 99 p., 1 pl. 8°.   **NBM**

—— Daphne; or, The pipes of Arcadia. Three acts of singing nonsense. New York: The Century Co., 1896. 5 p.l., 166 p., 6 pl. 16°.   **NBM**

—— Festival plays. One-act pieces for New Year's day, St. Valentine's day, Easter, All Hallowe'en, Christmas, and a child's birthday. New York: Duffield & Co,. 1913. 6 p.l., 9–302 p., 1 pl. 8°. **NBM**
Father Time and his children. Ternulla's garden; or, The miracle of good St. Valentine. The seven sleepers of Ephesos. Princess Moss Rose. The testing of Sir Gawayne. A Christmas party.

—— Picture plays. New York: Duffield and Company, 1911. 133 p., 4 pl., 3 port. 8°.   **NBM**
The last sitting. A salon carré fantasy. His mother's face. A Gainsborough lady. Artist-mother and child. Queen and emperor. Millet group.

Merriman, Effie Woodward. The Bachelors' Club. ₁A drama.₎ Chicago: The Dramatic Publishing Company, cop. 1901. 30 p. 12°. NBL p.v.15, no.3

—— Diamonds and hearts. Comedy-drama in three acts. Chicago: The Dramatic Publishing Company ₁cop. 1897₎. 40 p. 12°. (Sergel's acting drama. no. 418.) NBL p.v.3, no.2

—— The Emerson Club. Comedy in one act. Chicago: The Dramatic Publishing Company ₁cop. 1901₎. 12 p. 12°. (American acting drama.) NBL p.v.15, no.6

—— A girl's secret. A play in three acts. Chicago: The Dramatic Pub. Co. ₁cop. 1901.₎ 29 p. 12°. (Sergel's acting drama. no. 467.) NBL p.v.4, no.9

—— The great Plummer breach-of-promise case. A mock trial. Chicago: The Dramatic Publishing Company ₁cop. 1902₎. 35 p. 12°. (Sergel's acting drama. no. 439.) NBL p.v.3, no.1

—— Maud Muller. A burlesque entertainment in three acts. Chicago: The Dramatic Publishing Company ₁cop. 1891₎. 63–88 p. 12°. (American amateur drama.) NBL p.v.17, no.4

—— The silent detective. A drama in three acts. Chicago: The Dramatic Publishing Company ₁cop. 1901₎. 43 p. 12°. (American acting drama.) NBL p.v.15, no.5

—— Tompkins' hired man. A drama in three acts. Chicago: The Dramatic Publishing Company ₁cop. 1898₎. 35 p. 12°. (Sergel's acting drama. no. 419.) NBL p.v.3, no.3

Merz, Charles Andrew, and F. W. Tuttle. Quentin Durward; a dramatic adaptation of Sir Walter Scott's novel, in three acts and three scenes. New Haven: Yale University Dramatic Association, 1914. 7 p.l., 7–92 p. 8°. NBM

Metcalfe, Irving. A game of chance; or, Allotting the bride. A comedy in one act. New York: The Dramatic Publishing Company ₁cop. 1899₎. 24 p. 16°. (The wizard series.) NBL p.v.22, no.4

—— Miss Mary Smith. A comedy in one act. New York: The Dramatic Publishing Company ₁cop. 1899₎. 21 p. 16°. (The wizard series.) NBL p.v.22, no.3

Meyer, Annie Nathan. The dominant sex; a play in three acts. New York: Brandu's, 1911. 4 p.l., 11–112 p. 12°. NBM

—— The dreamer; a play in three acts. New York: Broadway Pub. Co., 1912. 4 p.l., 112 p. 12°. NBM

Meyers, Robert Cornelius V. Cousin Tom: a comedietta in one act. Philadelphia: The Penn Publishing Co., 1908. 13 p. 12°. NBL p.v.6, no.9

Middleton, George. Embers; with, The failures, The gargoyle, In his house, Madonna, The man masterful. One-act plays of contemporary life. New York: Henry Holt and Company, 1911. 5 p.l., 3–192 p. 12°. NBM

—— The man masterful. (Forum. New York, 1909. 8°. v. 42, p. 369–382.) *DA

—— Nowadays; a contemporaneous comedy. New York: Henry Holt and Company, 1914. v, 218 p. 12°. NBM

—— Possession, with, The groove, The unborn, Circles, A good woman, The black tie; one-act plays of contemporary life. New York: Henry Holt and Company. 1915. ix p., 2 l., (1)4–217 p. 12°. NBM

—— Tradition, with, On bail, Their wife, Waiting, The cheat of pity, and Mothers; one-act plays of contemporary life. New York: Henry Holt and Company, 1913. 5 p.l., 3–173 p. 8°. NBM

Middleton, J. A. Red Sefchen: an incident in the life of Heinrich Heine. ₁Boston: J. W. Luce & Co., 1907.₎ 2 p.l., 23 p. 12°. NBI
Bound with his: Love songs and lyrics. Boston, 1907. 12°.

Miles, George Henry. Senor Valiente. A comedy. In five acts. Boston: W. V. Spencer, cop. 1858. 52 p. 12°. (Spencer's Boston theatre. no. 193.) NCOF
Prompter's copy, interleaved. With ms. notes.

The Military Glory of Great-Britain, an Entertainment, given by the late candidates for Bachelor's Degree, at the close of the anniversary commencement, held in Nassau-Hall, New-Jersey, September 29th, 1762. Philadelphia: Printed by William Bradford, 1762. 15 p., 5 pl. of music. 4°. Reserve

Miller, Chester Gore. Chihuahua. A new and original social drama in four acts. Chicago, Ill.: Kehm, Fietsch & Wilson Co., 1891. 95(1) p. 16°. NBM

—— Father Junipero Serra. A new and original historical drama, in four acts... Illustrated. Chicago: Skeen, Baker & Co., 1894. 160 p., 1 l., 1 port. 16°. NBM

Miller, Joaquin. The Danites in the Sierras: an idyl drama in four acts. San Francisco: The California Pub. Co., 1882. 101–203 p. 2. ed. 16°. NBM

—— Forty-nine: an idyl drama of the Sierras, in four acts. San Francisco: The California Pub. Co., 1882. 1 p.l., 102 p. 2. ed. 16°. NBM

—— '49 and the Danites. n. t.-p. ₁New York? pref. 1881.₎ 203 p. 16°. NBM

—— Joaquin Miller's poems. San Francisco: The Whitaker & Ray Co., 1909–10. 6 v. 12°. *R–NBI
v. 6 contains his dramas: The Danites in the Sierras, Forty-nine, Tally-ho, and An Oregon idyl.

Minshull, John. A comedy, entitled The sprightly widow, with the frolics of youth; or, A speedy way of uniting the sexes, by honorable marriage. New-York: printed for the author, 1803. vi p., 2 l., (1)12–64 p., 1 port. 8°.   **NBM**

—— A comic opera, entitled Rural felicity: with the humour of Patrick, and marriage of Shelty. New-York: printed for the author, 1801. viii p., 1 l., (1)12–68 p., 3 l., 1 port. 8°.   **NBM**

—— He stoops to conquer, or The virgin wife triumphant; a comedy in three acts. New-York: printed for the author, by G. & R. Waite, 1804. 33(1) p. 8°. **NBM**
Bound with his: A comedy entitled The sprightly widow. New-York, 1803. 8°.

—— The merry dames, or The humourist's triumph over the poet in petticoats, and the gallant exploits of the knight of the comb. A comedy in three acts. New-York: printed for the author, by G. & R. Waite, 1805. viii p., 1 l., (1)4–29(1) p. 8°.   **NBM**
Bound with his: A comedy entitled The sprightly widow. New-York, 1803. 8°.

Mitchell, Edmund. Her sacrifice; drama in prologue and three acts. Los Angeles, Cal.: Grafton Pub. Co., 1909. 20 l. 8°.
    NBL p.v.10, no.2

Mitchell, Langdon Elwyn. The New York idea; a comedy in four acts. Boston: W. H. Baker & Co., 1908. xii p., 1 l., 175 p. 12°.   **NBM**

Mitchell, Silas Weir. The complete poems of S. Weir Mitchell. New York: The Century Co., 1914. 6 p.l., 3–447 p. 12°.
    NBI
The dramatic poems included are Francis Drake, Philip Vernon, Responsibility, Wind and sea, A medal, The cup of youth, The violin, François Villon, The miser: a masque, The wager, and Barabbas.

—— A masque, and other poems. Boston: Houghton, Mifflin and Company, 1887. 4 p.l., 63 p. 8°.   **NBI**
A masque, p. 1–11.

—— Philip Vernon. A tale in prose and verse. New York: The Century Co., 1895. 1 p.l., 55 p. 12°.   **NBM**

—— The wager, and other poems. New York: The Century Co., 1900. 4 p.l., 47 p. 12°.   **NBI**
The wager, p. 1–14.

—— Wind and sea. (In his: The hill of stones, and other poems. Boston, 1883. 16°. p. 20–32.)   **NBI**

Monroe, Harriet. Valeria, and other poems. Chicago: A. C. McClurg & Company, 1892. xi p., 1 l., 3–301 p. 12°. **NBM**
Valeria: a tragedy, p. 1–194.

Monroe, J. R. Dramas and miscellaneous poems. Chicago: Knight & Leonard, prtrs., 1875. 190 p. 8°.   **NBM**
Argo and Irene, p. 44–80; Malachi and Miranda, p. 81–114.

Montenegro, Carlota. Alcestis. A drama [in verse]. Boston: The Poet Lore Co., 1909. 4 p.l., 7–110 p. 12°.   **NBM**

Moody, William Vaughn. The faith healer: a play in four acts. Boston: Houghton Mifflin Co., 1909. 4 p.l., (1)4–160 p., 1 l. 12°.   **NBM**

—— The fire-bringer. Boston: Houghton, Mifflin & Co., 1904. 4 p.l., 108 p. 12°.   **NBM**

—— The great divide: a play in three acts. New York: Macmillan Company, 1909. 4 p.l., (1)4–167 p. 12°.   **NBM**
Also printed in T. H. Dickinson's *Chief contemporary dramatists*, p. 283–315.

—— The masque of judgment. A masque drama in five acts and a prelude. Boston: Houghton, Mifflin & Co., 1902. 3 p.l., 127 p. 12°.   **NBM**

—— The poems and plays of William Vaughn Moody; with an introduction by J. M. Manly. Boston: Houghton Mifflin Co., 1912. 2 v. port. 12°.   *** R – NBI**
v. 1. Poems and poetic dramas.
v. 2. Prose plays.
The poetic dramas are The fire-bringer, The masque of judgment, and The death of Eve (a fragment); the prose dramas are The great divide and The faith healer.

Moore, Bernard Francis. Captain Jack; or, The Irish outlaw. An original Irish drama in three acts. Boston: W. H. Baker & Co. [cop. 1889.] 40 p. 12°. (Baker's edition of plays.)
    NBM (Moore), p.v.1

—— Faugh-a-Ballagh; or, The wearing of the green. A romantic Irish play in three acts. Boston: W. H. Baker & Co., 1899. 39 p. 12°. (Baker's edition of plays.)   **NBM (Moore), p.v.1**

—— The Irish agent. A play of Irish life in four acts. Boston: W. H. Baker & Co. [cop. 1889.] 41 p. 12°. (Baker's edition of plays.)   **NBM (Moore), p.v.1**

—— The Irish rebel. A romantic play of the days of '98, in three acts. Boston: W. H. Baker & Co., 1903. 38 p. 12°. (Baker's edition of plays.)
    NBM (Moore), p.v.1

—— The king of the Philippines. A farce comedy in three acts. Boston: W. H. Baker & Co., 1901. 47 p. 12°. (Baker's edition of plays.)   **NBM (Moore), p.v.1**

—— Poverty Flats. A play of western life in three acts. Boston: W. H. Baker & Co., 1899. 35 p. 12°. (Baker's edition of plays.)   **NBM (Moore), p.v.1**

—— Suzette. A farce-comedy in three acts. Boston: W. H. Baker & Co., 1903. 47 p. 12°. (Baker's edition of plays.)
    NBL p.v.15, no.4

—— The weeping willows. A romantic play in three acts. Boston: W. H. Baker & Co., 1903. 53 p. 12°. (Baker's edition of plays.)   **NBM (Moore), p.v.1**

Moore, Charles Leonard. Banquet of
Palacios: a comedy. Philadelphia: C. L.
Moore, 1889. 196 p. 16°.   **NBM**

—— Ghost of Rosalys; a play. Philadelphia: the author, 1900. 3 p.l., 9–174 p.
12°.   **NBL p.v. 23, no.2**

Moos, H. M. Mortara; or, The pope and
his inquisitors. A drama, together with
choice poems. Cincinnati: Bloch & Co.,
1860. 171 p. 16°.   *** PSQ**

Morris, George Pope. The maid of Sax-
ony: or, Who's the traitor? An opera in
three acts. (In his: Poems. New York,
1854. 3. ed. 8°. p. 247–350.)   **NBI**

Morrison, George Austin, the younger.
"La Fayette"; or, "The maid and the
marquis," an original burlesque in three
acts. New York: [A. E. Chasmar & Co.,]
1890. 86 p. 8°.   **NBM**

Morse, Northrop. Peach bloom: an
original play in four acts. New York:
Sociological Fund, Medical Review of Re-
views, 1913. 5 p.l., 184 p. 12°.   **NBM**

Morse, Woolson. Madam Piper, a musical melange. Music composed and play
concocted by Woolson Morse... Assist-
ed at times in the stirring by J. C. Good-
win... New York: The Art Interchange
Press, 1884. 35 p., 1 pl. 8°.
                        NBL p.v.10, no.12

Morton, John Maddison. Betsy Baker;
or, Too attentive by half. A farce in one
act. Philadelphia: The Penn Pub. Co.,
1900. 20 p. 12°.   **NBL p.v.20, no.6**

—— The sentinel. A musical burletta,
in one act. Boston, 1852. 35 l. f°.
                            † NCOF
Manuscript promptbook.

Moses, Mrs. A. J. Esther. A drama in
five acts. Cincinnati: Bloch Pub. Co., 1887.
27 p. 8°.   *** PSQ**

Mueller, Arthur W.? Stultitia; a nightmare and an awakening, in four discus-
sions, by a former American government
official [Arthur W. Mueller?]. New York:
F. A. Stokes Co. [1915.] 4 p.l., [vii]–viii, 180
p., 1 pl. 12°.   **NBM**

Mumford, Edward. Bargain day at
Bloomstein's; an entertainment in one act.
Philadelphia: Penn Pub. Co., 1913. 28 p.
12°.   **NBL p.v.32, no.5**

—— A square deal; a comedy in one act.
Philadelphia: Penn Pub. Co., 1912. 24 p.
12°.   **NBL p.v.32, no.10**

Munford, William. Poems, and com-
positions in prose on several occasions.
Richmond: printed by Samuel Pleasants,
Jun., 1798. 3 p.l., (1)6–189(1) p. 8°.
                          Reserve
Almoran and Hamet, p. 25–107.

Munn, Margaret Crosby. Will Shakespeare of Stratford and London. A drama
in four acts. New York: Dodd, Mead &
Co., 1910. 6 p.l., 351 p. 12°.   *** NCLF**

Murphy, Fitzgerald. A bit o' blarney.
An Irish play of the present time. In
three acts. Boston: W. H. Baker & Co.
[cop. 1893.] 42 p. 12°. (Baker's edition
of plays.)   **NBL p.v.20, no.5**

Musselman, N. H. Mila Whendle. An
"unpleasant play." (Poet lore. Boston,
1901. 8°. v. 13, p. 22–53.)   *** DA**

My aunt; a petit comedy... Philadelphia: C. Neal [18—?]. 27 p. 24°. (C. Neal's
edition.)   **NCOF**
Prompter's copy, interleaved. With ms. notes.

Nack, James. The immortal; a dramatic
romance; and other poems; With a memoir
of the author, by George P. Morris. New
York: Stringer and Townsend, 1850. vi,
172 p. 12°.   **NBHD**
The immortal, p. 15–83.

—— The spirit of vengeance. A drama,
in three acts. (In his: The romance of
the ring, and other poems. New York,
1859. 12°. p. 37–90.)   **NBI**

Najac, Émile de, and J. M. LANDER. The
scarlet letter. An American tragedy in
five acts, founded on Hawthorne's story,
dramatized by Count de Najac and J. M.
Lander. 1877. f°.   **† NCOF**
With three pamphlets containing the part of Hes-
ter Prynne; and the musical score on loose sheets.
Prompter's manuscript copy.

Nash, Joseph. Josephine; an historical
drama, in four acts. Boston: F. Wood,
prtr., 1874. 60 p. 16°.   **NBL p.v.20, no.4**

Nathan, Robert Gruntal. Atoms; a one
act play. (Harvard monthly. Cambridge,
Mass., 1913. 8°. v. 57, p. 31–38.)   **STG**

—— The coward. [A play in one act.]
(Harvard monthly. Cambridge, Mass.,
1914. 8°. v. 58, p. 20–28.)   **STG**

Nature and philosophy; or, The youth
who never saw a woman. A farce, in one
act... New York: Samuel French [185–?].
16 p. 12°. (French's minor drama; the
acting edition. no. 185.)   **NCOF**
Prompter's copy, interleaved. With ms. notes.

Neal, John. Otho: a tragedy, in five
acts. Boston: West, Richardson & Lord,
1819. xxi p., 2 l., 25–120 p. 16°. **NBM p.v.9**

Neall, Walter H. Before the war: a
musical comedy in one act. Philadelphia:
The Penn Publishing Co., 1908. 13 p. 12°.
                        NBL p.v.6, no.7

Neihardt, John Gneisenau. Eight hundred rubles. (Forum. New York, 1915.
8°. v. 53, p. 393–402.)   *** DA**

Newton, Charles E. Cast upon the
world. An entirely original drama, in five
acts... Chicago: The Dramatic Publishing Company, cop. 1869. 40 p. 12°.
(Sergel's acting drama. no. 175.)
                        NBL p.v.4, no.6

—— Out at sea. An entirely original
romantic drama, in a prologue and four

acts. New York: The Dramatic Publishing Company ₍cop. 1872₎. 40 p. 12°. (De Witt's acting plays. no. 178.)
NBL p.v.26, no.7

Newton, Harry L. The Booster Club of Blackville. A colored comedy concoction. Chicago: T. S. Denison ₍1907₎. 15 p. 12°. (Denison's acting plays.)
NBL p.v.6, no.17

—— A call to arms. A military comedietta in one act. Boston: W. H. Baker & Co., 1904. 14 p. 12°. (Vaudeville stage.)
NBL p.v.1, no.18

—— Donovan and the dago. A comedy sketch in one act. Philadelphia: Penn Pub. Co., 1904. 12 p. 12°. **NBL p.v.1, no.6**

—— Her second time on earth. A comedy sketch in one act. Boston: W. H. Baker & Co., 1904. 13 p. 12°. (Vaudeville stage.)
NBL p.v.1, no.20

—— The little red school-house. A burlesque sketch on education for a singing quartette. Chicago: T. S. Denison ₍cop. 1908₎. 8 p. 12°. (Denison's vaudeville sketches.)
NBL p.v.8, no.20

—— Look out for the cat. A sketch in one act for two black-face comedians. Boston: W. H. Baker & Co., 1904. 12 p. 12°. (Vaudeville stage.) **NBL p.v.1, no.16a**

—— Mr. and Mrs. Fido. A vaudeville sketch. Chicago: T. S. Denison ₍1907₎. 10 p. 12°. (Denison's acting plays.) **NBL**

—— Oshkosh next week. A comedy for a singing quartette. Chicago: T. S. Denison ₍cop. 1908₎. 7 p. 12°. (Denison's vaudeville sketches.)
NBL p.v.8, no.10

—— Pilsner and Poppyseed the two German gazabos. A sketch in one act. Boston: W. H. Baker & Co., 1904. 11 p. 12°. (Vaudeville stage.) **NBL p.v.1, no.19**

—— Strenuous Mame the Bowery girl. A vaudeville cocktail. Boston: W. H. Baker & Co., 1904. 13 p. 12°. (Vaudeville stage.)
NBL p.v.1, no.17

—— Two jay detectives. A rural riot of comedy. Chicago: T. S. Denison ₍cop. 1908₎. 9 p. 12°. (Denison's vaudeville sketches.)
NBL p.v.8, no.14

Newton, Harry L., and J. P. Roche. The heiress of Hoetown. A rural comedy in three acts. Chicago: T. S. Denison ₍cop. 1908₎. 55 p. 12°. (Alta series.)
NBL p.v.8, no.19

Nickles, Alice Belmer. The sixteenth century conflict. A study of the life of Dr. Martin Luther in dialogue. Philadelphia: The Lutheran Publication Society ₍cop. 1910₎. 43 p. 8°. **NBL p.v.24, no.3**

—— A study of St. Paul in dialogue. Philadelphia: The Lutheran Publication Society ₍cop. 1910₎. 74 p., 1 l. 8°.
NBL p.v.24, no.1

Nirdlinger, Charles Frederic. The first lady of the land; a play in four acts. Boston: W. H. Baker & Co., 1914. 209 p. 12°. **NBM**

—— The world and his wife. ₍A drama₎ after the verse of José Echegaray's El gran Galeoto. New York: Mitchell Kennerley ₍1908₎. 215 p., 6 pl. 8°. **NBM**

Noah, Mordecai Manuel. The fortress of Sorrento: a petit historical drama, in two acts. New York: D. Longworth, 1808. 28 p. 16°. **NBM p.v.7**

—— The Grecian captive, or The fall of Athens. New York: E. M. Murden, 1822. 2 p.l., ₍iii₎–iv, 48 p. 16°. **NBM p.v.7**

—— She would be a soldier, or The plains of Chippewa; an historical drama, in three acts. New York: G. L. Birch & Co., 1819. 1 p.l., 5–73 p. 16°. **NBM**
p. 3–4 lacking.

Nobles, Milton. The phœnix: a drama in four acts. Chicago: Drama Pub. Co., 1900. 3 p.l., 128 p. 12°. **NBL p.v.14, no.9**

Northall, William Knight. Macbeth travestie: with the stage business... New York: W. Taylor & Co., 1847. 2 p.l., (1)8–36 p. 12°. *** NCN p.v.4, no.11**

Norton, Allen. The convolvulus; a comedy in three acts. New York: Claire Marie, 1915. 72 p. 12°. **NBM**

Norton, Franklin P. Six dramas of American romance and history. New York: Schulte Press, 1915. 2 p.l., (1)8–209 p., 1 port. 4°. **NBM**
The secretary of state. Financier of New York. Abraham Lincoln. Otomis, the Indian of Mexico. The third term. King of Wall Street.

Norton, Louise. Little wax candle; a farce in one act. New York: Claire Marie, 1914. 38 p. 12°. **NBM**

O'Brien, William L. Aaron Burr: a play in four acts. ₍Minneapolis, Minn.: Review Pub. Co., 1908.₎ 82 p. 8°.
NBL p.v.10, no.11

Ochs, Julius. The Megilla; or, The story of Esther: an operatic medley. Cincinnati: Bloch Pub. & Print. Co. ₍19—?₎ 32 p. 12°. *** PSQ**

O'Conor, John Francis Xavier. "Everysoul" and the Land of the Sunrise Sea; operetta. A mystery play and musical drama. Words and music by J. F. X. O'Conor. ₍New York: J. Lane Co., cop. 1913.₎ .71(1) p., 3 pl. 4. ed. 12°. *** MZ**

Oliver, Roland. Little Face. ₍A drama of the prehistoric era.₎ (Smart set. New York, 1914. 8°. v. 44, p. 131–141.) **NBA**

102; or, The veteran and his progeny. Boston: Richardson & Lord, 1828. 33 p. 16°. **NBM p.v.5**

O'Neill, Eugene Gladstone. Thirst, and other one act plays. Boston: Gorham

Press ₁1914₁. 168 p. 12°. (American dramatists series.) **NBM**
Thirst. The web. Warnings. Fog. Recklessness.

Opal, pseud. The cloud of witnesses. New York: J. Miller, 1874. 522 p. 12°. **NBM**

Oppenheim, James. The pioneers: a poetic drama in two scenes. New York: B. W. Huebsch, 1910. 61 p. 12°. **NBM**

Orne, M. R. A limb o' the law. A comedy in two acts. Boston: W. H. Baker & Co. ₁cop. 1892.₁ 18 p. 12°. (Baker's edition of plays.) **NBL** p.v.17, no.12

Orton, Jason Rockwood. Arnold, and other poems. New York: Partridge & Brittan, 1854. 144 p. 12°. **NBM**
Arnold, p. 7–101.

Osborn, Laughton. Bianca Capello; a tragedy, being in completion of the first volume of the dramatic series. New York: Moorhead, Simpson & Bond, 1868. 2 p.l., (1)204–419 p. 12°. **NBM**

—— Calvary — Virginia; tragedies. New York: Doolady, 1867. 4 p.l., 200 p. 12°. **NBM**

—— Dramatic works. v. 1–2, 4. New York, 1868–70. 12°. **NBM**
v. 1 and 4 have imprint, New York: James Miller, 1868; v. 2 has imprint, New York: The American News Company, 1870.
v. 1. Calvary, Virginia, Bianca Capello.
v. 2. Ugo da Este, Uberto, The Cid of Seville, The last Mandeville, The heart's sacrifice, The monk, Matilda of Denmark.
v. 4. The silver head, The double deceit, The Montanini, The school for critics.

—— The last Mandeville, The heart's sacrifice, The monk, Matilda of Denmark; tragedies, being in completion of the second volume of the dramatic series. New York: The American News Company, 1870. 2 p.l., (1)274–605(1) p. 12°. **NBM**

—— Mariamne, being the third of the tragedies of Jewish and Biblical history, and the second in continuation of volume vi of the dramatic series. New York: H. L. Hinton, 1873. 2 p.l., 167–269 p. 8°. ***PSQ**

—— The Montanini: a comedy, being in continuation of the fourth volume of the dramatic series. New York: James Miller, 1868. 2 p.l., (1) 266–397 p. 12°. **NBL** p.v.11, no.10

—— The silver head, The double deceit; comedies. New York: Doolady, 1867. 262 p., 1 l. 8°. **NBM**

—— Ugo da Este — Uberto — The Cid of Seville; tragedies. New York: James Miller, 1869. 269 p. 12°. **NBM**

Osborne, Duffield. Xanthippe on woman suffrage; dialogue. (Yale review. New Haven, 1915. 8°. v. 4, p. 590–607.) ***DA**

Osborne, Harry W. A home run. A vaudeville sketch. Chicago: T. S. Denison ₁cop. 1908₁. 9 p. 12°. (Denison's vaudeville sketches.) **NBL** p.v.8, no.21

Osgood, Harry O. The Bigelows' butler. A comedy in three acts. Boston: W. H. Baker & Co., 1903. 62 p. 12°. (Baker's edition of plays.) **NBL** p.v.17, no.18

—— Mrs. Compton's manager. A comedy in three acts. Boston: W. H. Baker & Co. ₁cop. 1902.₁ 58 p. 12°. (Baker's edition of plays.) **NBL** p.v.18, no.23

Osgood, L. W. The Union spy; or, The battle of Weldon railroad. A military drama in five acts. Woburn, Mass.: J. L. Parker, 1871. 32 p. 16°. (Parker's amateur player.) **NBL** p.v.26, no.1

Out of place; or, The lake of Lausanne; a musical farce, in two acts. New York: W. Turner, 1808. 41 p. 24°. **NCO** p.v.292

Owen, Robert Dale. Pocahontas: a historical drama, in five acts; with an introductory essay and notes. By a citizen of the West ₁i.e., Robert Dale Owen₁. New York: George Dearborn, 1837. 2 p.l., (1)8–240 p. 12°. **NBM**

Paine, Thomas. A dialogue between the ghost of General Montgomery just arrived from the Elysian fields; and an American delegate, in a wood near Philadelphia. ₁By Thomas Paine.₁ ₁Philadelphia:₁ Printed, and sold by R. Bell, 1776. New York: privately reprinted, 1865. 3 p.l., (1)6–16 p. 8°. **IGA**

Painton, Edith F. A. U. Palmer. The healing touch; a drama in four acts. New York: Shakespeare Press, 1914. 92 p., 1 l. 12°. **NBM**

Pallen, Condé Benoist. The feast of Thalarchus. A dramatic poem. Boston: Small, Maynard & Co., 1901. viii, 73 p. 12°. **NBM**

Palmer, John Williamson. The queen's heart. A comedy in three acts. ₁By J. W. Palmer.₁ Boston: W. V. Spencer, 1858. 80 p. 12°. **NCOF**
Prompter's copy, interleaved. With ms. notes.

Park, John Edgar. The dwarf's spell: a Christmas play. Boston ₁etc.₁: The Pilgrim Press ₁cop. 1912₁. 5 p.l., (1)4–55 p. 12°. **NBM**

Parke, John. Virginia: a pastoral drama, on the birth-day of an illustrious personage and the return of peace, February 11th, 1784. ₁By John Parke.₁ Philadelphia: Printed by Eleazer Oswald, at the Coffee-House, 1786. (In: Horace, The lyric works of Horace, translated into English verse. Philadelphia, 1786. 8°. p. 321–334.) **Reserve**

Parker, Lem B. Up Vermont way. A rural comedy drama in four acts. Chicago: The Dramatic Publishing Company ₍cop. 1903₎. 83 p. 12°. (Sergel's acting drama. no. 528.) **NBL p.v.3, no.4**

Parker, Mary Moncure. Mrs. Busby's pink tea. A comedy in one act. Chicago: The Dramatic Publishing Company ₍cop. 1902₎. 10 p. 12°. (Sergel's acting drama. no. 438.) **NBL p.v.3, no.5**

Parker, Maud May. The missive. A dramatic poem. Boston: The Poet Lore Co., 1907. 48 p. 12°. **NBM**

Parker, W. C. The face at the window. A drama in three acts. Chicago: T. S. Denison ₍1904₎. 39 p. 12°. (Alta series.) **NBL p.v.1, no.21**

—— A friend of the whole family. A farce comedy in three acts. Chicago: T. S. Denison ₍1904₎. 36 p. 12°. (Alta series.) **NBL p.v.1, no.23**

—— His second time on earth. A farce comedy in three acts. Chicago: T. S.. Denison ₍1904₎. 47 p. 12°. (Alta series.) **NBL p.v.1, no.24**

—— Love and anarchy. A sensational melodrama in four acts. Chicago: T. S. Denison ₍1904₎. 50 p. 12°. (Alta series.) **NBL p.v.1, no.22**

—— Second childhood. A farce in one act. Chicago: T. S. Denison ₍cop. 1908₎. 11 p. 12°. (Amateur series.) **NBL p.v.8, no.16**

—— Those red envelopes. A farce in one act. Chicago: T. S. Denison ₍cop. 1908₎. 14 p. 12°. (Amateur series.) **NBL p.v.8, no.12**

Parsons, George Sanford, and A. R. ALLEN. Princess Proud. A comic opera, in two acts. Book by G. S. Parsons, and A. R. Allen, with music by G. S. Parsons. Presented by the Columbia University Musical Society...February...1901. ₍New York, 1901₎ 48 p. illus. 4°. **†NBM**

Patten, Gilbert. In double peril. (Near Gettysburg, '63.) A semi-military drama of the Civil war, in three acts. Adapted from the French. Boston: W. H. Baker & Co., 1903. 58 p. 12°. **NBL p.v.18, no.24**

Paul Forrester: a play in four acts. New York, 1871. 110 p., 1 l. 8°. **NBM**

Paulding, James Kirke, and W. I. PAULDING. American comedies... Philadelphia: Carey and Hart, 1847. 2 p.l., ₍iii₎–iv p., 1 l., (1)17–295 p. 12°. **NBM**
The Bucktails; or, Americans in England, by J. K. Paulding. The noble exile, Madmen all, and Antipathies, by W. I. Paulding.

The **Paxton** Boys, a Farce. Translated from the Original French, By a Native of Donegal. Printed in the Year, MDCCLXIV. 16 p. 16°. **Reserve**

Payne, John Howard. Accusation; or, The family of D'Anglade: a melo drama, in three acts... Boston: West, Richardson & Lord, 1818. vii(i), (1)10–76 p. 16°. **NBM p.v.11**

—— Adeline, the victim of seduction: a melo-dramatic serious drama, in three acts: altered from the French of Monsieur R. C. Guilbert Pixerècourt, and adapted to the English stage: by John Howard Payne ... London: Theatre Royal, Drury Lane ₍J. Tabby, prtr.₎, 1822. 42 p. 12°. **NCO p.v.154, no.3**

—— Ali Pacha; or, The signet-ring. A melodrama, in two acts... New York: E. M. Murden, 1823. 36 p. 16°. **NCOF**
Prompter's copy, interleaved. With ms. notes.

—— Brutus; or, The fall of Tarquin. An historical tragedy, in five acts. London: T. Rodwell, 1818. viii, 58 p. 5. ed. 8°. **NCO p.v.219**

—— —— New-York: D. Longworth, 1819. 54 p. 16°. **NCOF**
p. 45–46 lacking.
Prompter's copy, interleaved; with ms. notes.

—— —— New-York: Thomas Longworth, 1821. vi, (1)8–54 p. 16°. **NBM p.v.11**

—— —— London: G. H. Davidson ₍18—?₎. 4 p., 1 l., vii–viii, 9–52 p. 24° bd. as sq. 8°. **NCOF**
Prompter's copy, interleaved; with ms. notes.

—— —— New York: W. Taylor & Co. ₍18—?₎ v, 6–53 p. 12°. (Modern standard drama. no. 59.) **NCOF**
Prompter's copy, interleaved. With ms. notes.

—— Charles the Second: or, The merry monarch. A comedy, in two acts. New York: S. French ₍18—?₎. 1 p.l., 7–44 p. 12°. (French's standard drama. no. 19.) **NBL p.v.17, no.17**

—— —— London: T. H. Lacy ₍18—?₎. 40 p. 12°. (Lacy's acting edition of plays. v. 30.) **NCO**

—— Clari; or, The maid of Milan. A drama, in three acts...and a memoir of W. H. (Sedley) Smith. New York: S. French ₍18—?₎. 24 p. 12°. (French's standard drama. no. 259.) **NBL p.v.5, no.19**

—— —— London: John Miller, 1823. 2 p.l., 45 p. 8°. **NCO p.v.187**

—— Clari, the maid of Milan! A musical drama, in two acts... Music by Bishop. London: T. H. Lacy ₍18—?₎. 40 p. illus. 12°. (Lacy's acting edition of plays. v. 95.) **NCO**

—— Clari; or, The maid of Milan: an opera. London: J. Cumberland ₍18—?₎. 40 p. 24°. **NBH p.v.31, no.6**

—— —— Philadelphia: F. Turner ₍18—?₎. 4 p.l., 13–40 p., 1 pl. 16°. (Turner's dramatic library.) **NCOF**
Prompter's copy, interleaved. With ms. notes.

—— Julia, or The wanderer; a comedy, in five acts... New-York: D. Longworth. 1806. 2 p.l., (1)8–70 p., 1 l. 12°. **NBM p.v.11**

—— Love in humble life. A drama, in one act, adapted from Scribe and Dupin's "Michael et Christine." By John Howard Payne. London: T. H. Lacy ₁1822?₁. 24 p. 16°. (Lacy's acting edition of plays. v. 21.) **NCO**

—— Lovers' vows; a play, in five acts ... Baltimore: Geo. Dobbin and Murphy, 1809. vii(i), (1)10–90 p., 1 l. 12°. **NBM p.v.11**

—— Mrs. Smith; or, The wife and the widow. A farce... London: T. H. Lacy ₁18—?₁. 20 p. 12°. (Lacy's acting edition of plays. v. 84.) **NCO**

—— Payne's tragedy of Brutus; or, The fall of Tarquin. As presented by Edwin Booth. Boston: C. H. Thayer ₁cop. 1878₁. 84 p. 16°. (Dramatic library. v. 1, no. 9.) **NBL p.v.27, no.4**

—— Peter Smink; or, The armistice. A comic drama, in one act. Adapted from the French. London: T. H. Lacy ₁18—?₁. 16 p. 12°. (Lacy's acting edition of plays. v. 75.) **NCO**

—— Thérése, the orphan of Geneva, a drama, in three acts... New-York: Thomas Longworth, 1821. 7 p., 1 l., (1) 12–51 p. 16°. **NBM p.v.11**

—— —— New York: S. French ₁18—?₁. 33 p. 12°. **NCOF**
Prompter's copy, interleaved; with ms. notes.

—— —— London: Theatre Royal. 1821. viii, (1)10–57(1) p. 2. ed. 8°. **NCOF**

—— 'Twas I! A farce, in one act. London: T. H. Lacy ₁1825?₁. 15 p. 12°. (Lacy's acting edition. no. 128.) **NCOF**
Prompter's copy, interleaved. With ms. notes. The Library also has another prompter's copy with ms. notes.

—— The two galley slaves: a melodrama in two acts. Adapted from the French. London: T. H. Lacy ₁18—?₁. 29 p. 12°. (Lacy's acting edition of plays. v. 72.) **NCO**

—— —— London: J. Cumberland ₁18—?₁. 33 p. 24°. **NCOF**
Prompter's copy, interleaved. With ms. notes.

Peabody, Josephine Preston. Fortune and men's eyes: new poems with a play. Boston: Houghton Mifflin Co. ₁cop. 1900.₁ viii, 111(1) p. 12°. **NBM**
One of 750 copies printed.
Fortune and men's eyes: a drama in one act, p. 5–49.

—— Marlowe. A drama in five acts. Boston: Houghton, Mifflin & Co., 1901. 1 p.l., 156 p. 8°. **NBM**

—— The piper. A play in four acts. Boston: Houghton Mifflin Co., 1909. 6 p.l., (1)4–201(1) p. 8°. **NBM**

—— The wings. ₁A play in one act.₁ (Poet lore. Boston, 1914. 8°. v. 25, p. 352–369.) ***DA**

—— The wolf of Gubbio; a comedy in three acts. ₁In verse.₁ Boston: Houghton Mifflin Co., 1913. 6 p.l., (1)4–195(1) p. 8°. **NBM**

Penn, Arthur, pseud. See **Matthews,** James Brander.

Peterson, Henry. Cæsar; a dramatic study. In five acts. Philadelphia: H. Peterson & Co., 1879. 72 p. 12°. **NBM p.v.4**

Phillips, David Graham. The worth of a woman: a play in four acts. Followed by A point of law: a dramatic incident. New York: D. Appleton & Co., 1908. viii p., 2 l., 3–128 p. 12°. **NBM**

Phillips, Ida Orissa. The bright and dark sides of girl-life in India. Boston: Morning Star Publishing House, 1891. 32 p. 12°. **NBL p.v.1, no.7**

Phillips, John Franklyn. Honor. A family drama in three acts. New York: the author, 1909. 53 p. 12°. **NBM**
no. 19 of 33 copies printed.

Phillips, Jonas B. The evil eye. A melodrama in two acts... New York: S. French ₁1831₁. 16 p. 12°. (The minor drama. no. 134.) **NBM p.v.2**

—— Zamira, a dramatic sketch, and other poems. New-York: printed by G. A. C. Van Beuren, 1835. 142 p. 12°. **NBHD**
Zamira, a dramatic sketch, p. 7–19.

Pichel, Irving. Tom, Tom, the piper's son; an episode of character. (Harvard monthly. Cambridge, Mass., 1913. 8°. v. 57, p. 80–88.) **STG**

Pickett, Haskell. The rake's lesson; or, Taming a husband. A comic drama in two acts. ₁185–?₁ 88 l. 12°. **NCOF**
Manuscript promptbook.

Pierra, Adolfo. The Cuban patriots; a drama of the struggle for independence actually going on in the gem of the Antilles. In three acts. Written in English by a native Cuban ₁i.e., Adolfo Pierra₁. Philadelphia, 1873. iv p., 1 l., (1)8–45(1) p., 1 l. 16°. **NBL p.v.12, no.3**

Pilgrim, James. Eveleen Wilson, the flower of Erin; an original drama... Boston: W. V. Spencer ₁1853?₁. 32 p. 12°. (Spencer's Boston theatre. no. 77.) **NCOF**
Prompter's copy, interleaved. With ms. notes.

—— The female highwayman; or, The blighted lily. A drama in three acts. New York, 1852. 3 pamphlets. 4°. **NCOF**
Prompter's manuscript copy, made by E. S. Bowles.

—— Paddy Miles the Limerick boy. A farce, in one act. London: T. H. Lacy ₁18—?₁. 16 p. new ed., rev. 12°. (Lacy's acting edition of plays. v. 95.)   **NCO**

—— Yankee Jack; or, The buccaneer of the Gulf. A nautical drama in three acts. ₁18—?₁ 3 pamphlets. 4°.   † **NCOF**

Prompter's manuscript copy, made by E. S. Bowles.

Pine, M. S., pseud. of Sister Mary Paulina Finn. Alma mater; or, The Georgetown centennial, and other dramas. Published for Georgetown Visitation Convent. Washington, D. C., 1913. 254 p., 1 l. 8°.   **NBM**

Alma mater; or, The Georgetown centennial: a drama in three acts. Hermine: a drama in three acts. Hearts of gold, true and tried: a colonial drama in five acts. The Church's triumph. The angels' feast. The star of Bethlehem. The angels' meeting of Terra Mariae. A Georgetown reunion and what came of it.

Pleasant, Lillian. Their godfather from Paris; comedy in one act. New York: E. A. Fink ₁cop. 1905₁. 28 p. 12°.   **NBL p.v.27, no.10**

Ponte, Lorenzo da. Il Don Giovanni, dramma buffo, in due atti. La parte poetica della traduzione da L. da Ponte, jun. Nova-Jorca: Stampato da Giovanni Gray e Co., 1826. 95 p. 24°.   **NNO p.v.134, no.4**

Text in Italian and English.

—— Eliza and Claudio; or, Love protected by friendship. A melodrama... New York: for Lorenzo da Ponte, J. H. Turney, prtr., 1833. 2 p.l., (1)8–77(1) p. 2. ed. 16°.   **NCO p.v.248, no.4**

Text in Italian and English.

—— Il Mezenzio. Tragedia originale ... Nuova-Jorca: Joseph Desnoues, 1834. 77 p. 24°.   **NNR**

—— Le nozze di figaro, Il Don Giovanni, e L'Assur, re d'Ormus; tre drammi... New-York: Stampatori Giovanni Gray e Co., 1826. 1 p.l., ii, iv, (1)4–63, 51, 47 p. 24°.   **NNR**

Bound with his: Il Mezenzio. Nuova-Jorca, 1834. 24°.

Each drama also has a separate title-page.

Pratt, William W. Ten nights in a barroom. A drama, in five acts. Dramatized from T. S. Arthur's novel of the same name. Boston: W. H. Baker & Co. ₁cop. 1889.₁ 37 p. 12°. (Baker's edition of plays.)   **NBL p.v.17, no.16**

Pray, Isaac Clarke. Julietta Gordini, the miser's daughter. A play. ₁By I. C. Pray.₁ New York, 1839. 2 p.l., 3–40 p. 8°.   **NCOF**

Prompter's copy, interleaved. With ms. notes.

The **Prince** and the patriot: a poem, in three dialogues. (In: Poems, moral and divine... By an American gentleman. London, 1756. 4°. p. 79–105.)   **Reserve**

Putnam, Nina Wilcox. Orthodoxy. A play in one act. (Forum. New York, 1914. 8°. v. 51, p. 801–820.)   *** DA**

Quincy, Josiah Phillips. Charicles: a dramatic poem. By the author of Lyteria. Boston: Ticknor and Fields, 1856. 1 p.l., 5–106 p. 12°.   **NBI**

—— Lyteria. A dramatic poem. Boston: Ticknor & Fields, 1854. iv p., 1 l., (1) 8–123 p. 12°.   **NBM**

Quinn, Richard. Innisfail; or, The wanderer's dream. A drama of Irish life in four acts. Boston: W. H. Baker & Co. ₁cop. 1890.₁ 53 p. 12°. (Baker's edition of plays.)   **NBL p.v.17, no.14**

Raymond, George Lansing. The Aztec god, and other dramas. Third edition, abridged, with omitted passages printed in footnotes. New York: G. P. Putnam's Sons, 1908. iii, 446 p. 16°.   **NBM**

The Aztec god. Columbus. Cecil the seer.

—— Dante, and collected verse. New York: G. P. Putnam's Sons, 1909. vi, 329 p. 16°.   **NBI**

Dante, p. 5–127.

Read, Harriette Fanning. Dramatic poems. Boston: Wm. Crosby and H. P. Nichols, 1848. vi p., 3 l., 297 p., 1 fac. 8°.   **NBM**

Medea. Erminia; a tale of Florence. The New World.

—— Marie Antoinette. An historical play in five acts. Philadelphia, 1868. 6 pamphlets. f°.   † **NCOF**

Prompter's manuscript copy. The Library also has another prompter's copy, without the part of Marie Antoinette.

Rebecca and Rowena; or, The triumph of Israel. ₁A tragic burlesque in five acts.₁ n. t.-p. New York: C. B. Vaux, 1883. 28 p. 8°.   **NBL p.v.12, no.14**

Rebecca and Rowena; or, The triumph of Israel. A tragic burlesque in five acts —for amateur parlor representation— based on Thackeray's sequel to Ivanhoe. New York: C. B. Vaux, 1883. 28 p. 16°.   **NBL p.v.12, no.9**

—— New York: Roorbach & Co. ₁cop. 1883.₁ 28 p. 12°. (The acting drama. no. 185.)   **NBL p.v.9, no.5**

Rees, Arthur Dougherty. Columbus: a drama; with introduction and notes. Philadelphia: The J. C. Winston Co. ₁1907.₁ 2 p.l., 7–129 p., 1 pl. 12°.   **NBM**

—— The double love: a tragedy in five acts. A drama of American life. Philadelphia: J. C. Winston Co. ₁cop. 1907.₁ 85 p. 12°.   **NBM**

—— Give up your gods: a drama in three acts of pagan and Christian Russia. ₁In verse.₁ Philadelphia: J. B. Lippincott Co., 1908. 118 p., 1 l. 12°.   **NBM**

Rees, William Geulph. The mayor of Romanstown. A drama in three acts. New York: Cochrane Pub. Co., 1909. 73 p. 12°. **NBM**

The **Renegade.** A melodrama in four acts. [18—?] 4 pamphlets. f°. † **NCOF**
With the separate part of Athelstan, which is not included in the text.
Prompter's manuscript copy.

Requier, Augustus Julian. Marco Bozzaris. A play, in three acts. (In his: Poems. Philadelphia, 1860. 12°. p. 127–190.) **NBI**

Reynartz, Dorothy. A cup of coffee. Comedy in one act, for young ladies. Chicago: The Dramatic Publishing Company [cop. 1899]. 22 p. 12°. (Sergel's acting drama. no. 526.) **NBL p.v.3, no.6**

Rice, Cale Young. Collected plays and poems. Garden City: Doubleday, Page & Co., 1915. 2 v. port. 12°. **NBI**
The plays included are A night in Avignon, v. 1, p. 131–155; Yolanda of Cyprus, v. 1, p. 157–294; Porzia, v. 1, p. 549–633; Charles di Tocca, v. 2, p. 103–240; David, v. 2, p. 519–650.

—— David; a tragedy [in four acts and in verse]. New York: McClure, Phillips & Co., 1904. 3 p.l., [v]–vi, 118 p. 4°. **NBM**

—— A night in Avignon. [Drama in verse.] New York: McClure, Phillips & Co., 1907. 4 p.l., 3–32 p. 8°. **NBM**

—— Porzia. Garden City, N. Y.: Doubleday, Page & Co., 1913. viii, 79(1) p. 12°. **NBM**

—— Yolanda of Cyprus. [Drama in four acts and in verse.] New York: McClure Co., 1908. 3 p.l., (1)4–134 p. 12°. **NBM**

Rice, Charles. The three guardsmen; or, The queen, the cardinal, and the adventurer. A drama, in three acts, founded on Dumas' celebrated romance. New York: S. French [188–?]. 60 p. 12°. (French's standard drama. no. 139.) **NBL p.v.27, no.7**

Rice, Wallace, and T. W. STEVENS. The chaplet of Pan; a masque. Chicago: Stage Guild [1913?]. 22 l. 8°. **NBL p.v.28, no.6**

Ricord, Elizabeth Stryker. Zamba; or, The insurrection. A dramatic poem, in five acts. Cambridge: John Owen, 1842. 139 p. 16°. **NBH p.v.1**

Riley, James Whitcomb. The flying islands of the night. Indianapolis: Bowen-Merrill Co., 1892. 4 p.l., 88 p. 12°. **NBM**

Ritchie, Anna Cora Ogden Mowatt. Fashion; or, Life in New York. A comedy, in five acts. London: W. Newbery, 1850. 3 p.l., 62 p. 12°. bound as 8°. **NCOF**
Prompter's copy, interleaved. With ms. notes.

—— —— London: W. Newbery, 1850. 4 p.l., 62 p., 1 l., 1 port. 12°. **NCOF**
Prompter's copy, interleaved. With ms. notes.

—— Plays. Boston: Ticknor and Fields, 1855. 2 p.l., [iii]–iv p., 1 l., (1)10–60 p., 3 l., 62 p. new and rev. ed. 12°. **NBM**
Armand; or, The peer and the peasant. Fashion; or, Life in New York.

Rittenhouse, Laura J. The milkmaids' convention; burlesque entertainment. Chicago: Dramatic Pub. Co., cop. 1898. 22 p. 12°. **NBL p.v.17, no.15**

Rizy, F. X. O'Neil the Great: dramatic poem in two parts. [Hartford, cop. 1879.] 1 p.l., 16 p. 16°. **NBL p.v.22, no.11**

Roberts, Myrtle Glenn. The foot of the rainbow. [A play in three acts.] San Francisco: Paul Elder and Co. [1914.] 6 p.l., 5–45 p., 1 l. 8°. **NBM**

Robertson, John. Riego; or, The Spanish martyr. A tragedy in five acts. Richmond: P. D. Bernard, 1850. 1 p.l., vi, 7–106 p. 16°. **NBL p.v.20, no.2**

Robinson, Edwin Arlington. Van Zorn; a comedy in three acts. New York: Macmillan Co., 1914. 5 p.l., 3–164 p. 12°. **NBM**

Rogers, Daniel. The Knight of the Rum Bottle & Co.; or, The speechmakers. A musical farce in five acts. Respectfully dedicated to the managers of the New York Theatre, by the editor of the City-Hall Recorder [i.e., Daniel Rogers]. New York: D. Longworth, 1818. 16 p. 16°. **NBM p.v.8**

Rogers, James Webb. Madame Surratt. A drama in five acts. Washington, D. C.: Thomas J. Brashears, prtr., 1879. New York, reprinted: William Abbatt, 1912. 4 p.l., (1)8–161 p. 4°. (Magazine of history. extra no. 20.) **IAG**

Rogers, Margaret Douglas. The gift; a poetic drama. [In two acts.] Cincinnati: Stewart & Kidd Co., 1914. 47 p. 12°. **NBM**

Rogers, Robert. Ponteach: or, The Savages of America. A tragedy. [By Robert Rogers.] London: Printed for the Author; and Sold by J. Millan, 1766. 110 p. 8°. **Reserve**

Rogers, Robert Emmons. The boy Will. [A drama in one act.] (Harvard monthly. Cambridge, Mass., 1906. 8°. v. 43, p. 238–249.) **STG**
A drama of the boyhood life of William Shakespeare.

Rolt-Wheeler, Francis William. Nimrod; a drama. Boston: Lothrop, Lee and Shepard Co. [1912.] xi p., 1 l., 90 p. 12°. **NBM**

Roof, Katharine Metcalf. The white woman. 5 pl. (Craftsman. New York, 1907. v. 13, p. 245–256.) **MNA**

Rookwood. A drama in three acts. Philadelphia, 1849. 3 pamphlets. f°. † **NCOF**
Prompter's manuscript copy. With the parts of the different characters in ten pamphlets.

Ropp, Edwin Oliver. Pocahontas. By Tecumtha ⌐pseud. of E. O. Ropp⌐. Normal, Ill.: The Universal Publishing Co., 1906. 1 p.l., (1)6–90 p. 12°.   **NBM**

Rose, Con, the younger. "Dead Sea fruit." A comedy drama. In five acts, and eight tableaux. ⌐Washington,⌐ 1875. iv, 5–78 p. 12°.   **NBL p.v.23, no.5**

Rosener, George M. A successful failure; farce in one act. New York: Dick & Fitzgerald, 1912. 16 p. 12°.
                      NBL p.v.27, no.12

Rosenfeld, Sydney. The club friend; or, A fashionable physician. An original comedy in four acts. New York: The Dramatic Publishing Company ⌐cop. 1897⌐. 3 p.l., 89 p. 12°. (Green-room edition of copyrighted plays.)   **NBL p.v.23, no.1**

—— High C. A comedietta, in one act. Being a free adaptation from the German of M. A. Grandjean. New York: Dramatic Pub. Co., cop. 1875. 17 p. 12°. (De Witt's acting plays. no. 191.)   **NGB p.v.143, no.1**

—— Mr. X. A farce in one act. Chicago: The Dramatic Publishing Company, cop. 1875. 17 p. 12°. (Sergel's acting drama. no. 188.)   **NBL p.v.3, no.7**

—— A pair of shoes. A farce, in one act. New York: The Dramatic Publishing Company, cop. 1882. 12 p. 12°. (De Witt's acting plays. no. 305.)
                      NBL p.v.17, no.11

Rosett, Joshua. The middle class; a play in four acts. Baltimore: Phoenix Publishers ⌐1912⌐. iv, 124 p. 12°.   **NBM**

Rosetti, Joseph. Household affairs; or, A cause for divorce. Comedy in one act. New York: The Dramatic Publishing Company, cop. 1899. 1 p.l., 16 p. 16°. (The wizard series.)   **NBL p.v.22, no.7**

Roskoten, Robert. Carlotta; a tragedy in five acts. Peoria, Ill.: ⌐J. W. Franks & Sons,⌐ 1880. 5 p.l., (1)10–123 p. 8°. **NBM**

Ross, Clinton. The lady of the Blackfriars; or, The old play. Binghamton, N. Y.: C. Ross ⌐1909⌐. 34 p., 1 l. 8°.
                      NBL p.v.10, no.5

Ross, Joseph M. Phintias and Damon. Morristown, N. J.: C. D. Platt, 1897. 76 p. 24°.   **NBL p.v.22, no.1**

Royle, Edwin Milton. The squaw-man. An idyl of the ranch. (Cosmopolitan. New York, 1904. 8°. v. 37, p. 411–418.)
                      ***DA**

Ruge, Clara. On the road; a drama in one act. New York: Modern Library, 1913. 26 p., 1 l. 16°. (Modern library. ⌐v.⌐ 2.)   **NBL p.v.28, no.8**

Rush, James. Hamlet. A dramatic prelude, in five acts. Philadelphia: Key & Biddle, 1834. 122 p. 12°.   **NBM**

Ryan, Samuel E. O'Day, the alderman. A comedy drama in four acts. Boston: W. H. Baker & Co., 1901. 64 p. 12°. (Baker's edition of plays.)   **NBL p.v.17, no.13**

Salmonsen, Morris. We mortals. A play. Chicago: J. M. W. Jones, 1897. 2 p.l., 147 p. 12°.   **NBM**

Salome, the daughter of Herodias. A dramatic poem. New York: Putnam, 1862. 251 p. 12°.   ***PSQ**

Saltus, Francis Saltus. The witch of En-dor, and other poems. Buffalo: C. W. Moulton, 1891. 3 p.l., ⌐xvii⌐–xviii p., 1 l., 331 p., 1 port. 12°.   **NBI**
    The dramatic poems included are Carthage, Belshar-uzzar, and Lot's wife.

Samuels, Maurice V. The Florentines. A play. New York: Brentano's, 1904. 153 p. 12°.   **NBM**

Sanborn, Arthur W. The clerks of Kittery; a comedy in seven acts. Boston: W. H. Baker & Co. ⌐1912.⌐ 2 p.l., 77 p. 8°.
                      NBM

—— Young America in the hands of his friends; a political drama. Boston: J. H. West Company ⌐1904⌐. 82 p. 12°. **NBM**

Sander, Harold. Byrd and Hurd; or, A fair exchange. A farcical sketch in one act. New York: Dick & Fitzgerald, 1907. 22 p. 12°.   **NBL p.v.7, no.25**

—— My uncle from India. A farcical comedy in four acts. (From the German.) New York: Dick & Fitzgerald, 1907. 85 p. 12°.   **NBL p.v.7, no.24**

Sanford, Amelia. The ghost of an idea. A comedietta in one act and three scenes. Philadelphia: Penn Pub. Co., 1898. 13 p. 12°.   **NBL p.v.17, no.8**

Santayana, George. Lucifer. A theological tragedy. Chicago: H. S. Stone & Co., 1899. 4 p.l., 187 p., 1 l. 12°. **NBM**

Sappington, T. L. A dental engagement. A vaudeville farce in one act, with songs. Music by H. B. Vincent. New York: Dick & Fitzgerald, 1909. 15 p. 12°.
                      NBL p.v.7

Sargent, Epes. Songs of the sea, with other poems. Boston: James Munroe and Company, 1847. 208 p. 12°.   **NBHD**
    The candid critic, p. 159–194. The lampoon, p. 195–201.

—— Velasco. A tragedy, in five acts. New York: Harper & Brothers, 1839. 4 p.l., 13–110 p. 12°.   **NBM**
    The Library also has a prompter's copy, with ms. notes.

Sargent, Frederick Leroy. Omar and the rabbi. Fitzgerald's translation of the Rubaiyat of Omar Khayyam, and Browning's Rabbi Ben Ezra, arranged in dramatic form. Cambridge: Harvard Coöperative Society, 1909. 28 p. 16°.
                      NBL p.v.12, no.2

Saul. A dramatic sketch. (American monthly magazine. Boston, 1829. 8°. v. 1, no. 3, June, 1829, p. 200–203.) ***DA**

Saunders, Charles H. Butchers of Ghent; or, The council of blood. A grand spectacle in four acts, founded on a tale of the same name, translated from the French. Dramatized by C. H. Saunders. ₁18—?₁ 4 pamphlets. 4°. **†NCOF**

Prompter's manuscript copy. The Library also has the parts of the different characters in 16 pamphlets.

—— The North End caulker; or, The mechanic's oath. A story of Boston harbor and the Rio Grande. In three acts. By C. H. S. Boston, 1851. 3 pamphlets. 4°. **†NCOF**

Prompter's manuscript copy. With 25 pamphlets containing the parts of the different characters.

—— The pirate's legacy. A drama in two acts. ₁18—?₁ 2 pamphlets. 4°. **†NCOF**

Prompter's manuscript copy.

—— Rosina Meadows, the village maid; or, Temptations unveiled. A local domestic drama, in three acts... Adapted from the popular novel of that name by Wm. B. English... Boston: William V. Spencer ₁185–?₁. viii, (1)10–52 p. 12°. (Spencer's Boston theatre. no. 11.) **NCOF**

Prompter's copy, interleaved. With ms. notes.

Sauter, Edwin. The death of Gracchus. A tragedy. Saint Louis: ₁the author,₁ 1908. v. 75(1) p. 16°. **NBM**

One of 200 copies printed.

—— The faithless favorite. A mixed tragedy. To which is appended a collection of detached trifles entitled Schediasm. St. Louis: the author, 1905. 4 p.l., 238 p. 16°. **NBM**

—— The poisoners; or, As 'twas done in Italy. A tragedy. Saint Louis: the author, 1906. vi, 72 p. 24°. **NBM**

Savage, John. Sybil. A tragedy, in five acts. New York: J. B. Kirker, 1865. 105 p. 12°. **NBM**

—— —— (In his: Poems: lyrical, dramatic, and romantic. New York, 1870. 2. collected ed. 12°. p. 133–220.) **NBI**

Scheffauer, Herman George. The hollow head of Mars; a modern masque in four phases. London: Simpkin, Marshall, Hamilton, Kent & Co., 1915. 4 p.l., 80 p., 1 pl. 12°. **NBM**

Schenck, Frederic. Death and the dicers; a play in one act, adapted from "The pardoner's tale" by Chaucer. (Harvard monthly. Cambridge, Mass., 1909. 8°. v. 48, p. 195–206.) **STG**

Schnittkind, Henry Thomas. Shambles; a sketch of the present war. (Poet lore. Boston, 1914. 8°. v. 25, p. 559–571.) ***DA**

The **School** for politicians; or, Noncommittal. A comedy, in five acts. ₁Based on A. E. Scribe's "Bertrand et Raton; ou, L'art de conspirer."₁ New York: Carvill & Co., 1840. v p., 1 l., (1)10–179 p. 8°. **NBM**

Schoonmaker, Edwin Davies. The Americans. ₁In five acts and in verse.₁ New York: Mitchell Kennerley, 1913. 304 p. 12°. **NBM**

—— The Saxons. A drama of Christianity in the North. Chicago, Ill.: The Hammersmark Pub. Co., 1905. 214 p. 8°. **NBM**

Schuetze, Martin. Hero and Leander: a tragedy. ₁In verse.₁ New York: Henry Holt and Co., 1908. 5 p.l., 7–176 p. 12°. **NBM**

—— Judith: a tragedy in five acts. ₁In verse.₁ New York: Henry Holt and Co., 1910. 5 p.l., 5–306 p. 8°. **NBM**

Scott, W. Atkins. Cupid in shirt sleeves. A...comedy in one act. New York: The Dramatic Publishing Company ₁cop. 1899₁. 18 p. 16°. (The wizard series.) **NBL p.v.22, no.8**

The **Sea** of ice; or, A thirst for gold, and the wild flower of Mexico. A romantic drama in five tableaux. New York: S. French ₁18—?₁. 40 p. 12°. (French's American drama; acting edition. no. 114.) **NCOF**

The Library has two prompter's copies of this edition, both with ms. notes.

—— —— New York: S. French ₁18—?₁. 40 p. 12°. (French's American drama. no. 30.) **NBM p.v.2**

Seaman, Abel. In the trenches. A drama of the Cuban war in three acts. Boston: W. H. Baker & Co., 1898. 37 p. 12°. (Baker's edition of plays.) **NBL p.v.17, no.9**

Sewall, Jonathan Mitchell. A Cure for the Spleen. or Amusement for a Winter's Evening; Being the Substance of a Conversation on the Times, over A Friendly Tankard and Pipe. between Sharp, a Country Parson, Pumper, A Country Justice, Fillpot, an Inn-Keeper, Graveairs, a Deacon, Trim, a Barber, Brim, a Quaker, Puff, a late Representative. Taken in short Hand, by Sir Roger De Coverly. ₁By Jonathan M. Sewall.₁ America: Printed and sold in the Year 1775. 32 p. 12°. **Reserve**

—— The Americans Roused in a Cure for the Spleen; or, Amusement for a Winter's Evening ₁remainder of title as in previous entry₁. New-England, Printed; New-York, Re-printed, by James Rivington ₁1775₁. 32 p. 8°. **Reserve**

Seymour, Harry. Aunt Dinah's pledge. A temperance drama, in two acts. Dramatized by permission of the National Temperance Society... New York: Happy Hours Co. ₁18—?₁ 19 p. new ed. 12°. (The acting drama. no. 57.) **NBL p.v.5, no.11**

—— —— Chicago: The Dramatic Publishing Company [189–?]. 18 p. 12°. Sergel's acting drama. no. 258.)
NBL p.v.3, no.8

Shaler, Nathaniel Southgate. Elizabeth of England. A dramatic romance in five parts. [Boston: Houghton, Mifflin & Co., 1903.] 5 v. 8°. **NBM**

v. 1. The coronation. v. 2. The rival queens. v. 3. Armada days. v. 4. The death of Essex. v. 5. The passing of the queen.

Shaw, Alexander Wilson. The girl in the picture; a play in two acts. Boston: Gorham Press [1914]. 4 p.l., 5–87 p. 12°. (American dramatists series.) **NBM**

Sheldon, Edward Brewster. The garden of paradise. Based on "The little mermaid" by Hans Andersen. New York: The Macmillan Company, 1915. xi p., 1 l., 244 p., 1 pl. 12°. **NBM**

—— "The nigger." An American play in three acts. New York: The Macmillan Co., 1910. 6 p.l., 3–269 p. 12°. **NBM**

—— Romance. New York: The Macmillan Company, 1914. xi p., 1 l., 232 p., 1 pl. 12°. **NBM**

Shields, C. Woodruff. The reformer of Geneva. An historical drama. New York: G. P. Putnam's Sons, 1898. 2 p.l., 125 p. 8°. **NBM**

Shields, Lottie. Kate's infatuation. A comedy in one act, for young ladies. New York: The Dramatic Publishing Company [cop. 1899]. 16 p. 16°. (The wizard series.) **NBL p.v.20, no.9**

Siege of Boston; or, The conspiracy. [A drama in five acts.] [18—?] 5 p.l., 3–65 p. f°. **†NCOF**

Manuscript promptbook.

Silver, W. A. Clouds. An original American comedy, in four acts. By Fred Marsden [pseud.]. New York: R. M. De Witt, cop. 1873. 64 p. 12°. **NCOF**

Prompter's copy, interleaved. With ms. notes.

Simmie, pseud. Antony and Hero. [A drama.] New Haven, Conn.: F. Simon, 1899. 61 p. 12°. **NBM**

Simms, William Gilmore. Atalantis; a story of the sea. Philadelphia: Carey and Hart, 1848. vi p., 1 l., 144 p. 12°. **NBM**

Atalantis occupies the first 72 p.

—— Norman Maurice; or, The man of the people. An American drama. In five acts. Richmond: Jno. R. Thompson, 1851. 31(1) p. 8°. **NBM**

—— Poems, descriptive, dramatic, legendary, and contemplative. New York: Redfield, 1853. 2 v. 12°. **NBI**

Norman Maurice; or, The man of the people, v. 1, p. 5–120. Atalantis; a story of the sea, v. 1, p. 123–208. Caius Marius, v. 2, p. 300–311. Bertram: an Italian sketch, v. 2, p. 312–328. The death of Cleopatra, v. 2, p. 329–333.

Sinclair, Upton Beall, the younger. Plays of protest. The naturewoman. The machine. The second-story man. Prince Hagen. New York: Mitchell Kennerley, 1912. 3 p.l., vi, 266 p. 12°. **NBM**

The **Sleeping** beauty; or, A tale of enchantment. [In two acts.] As produced at the National Theatre, Boston, Feb. 5, 1848. 2 p.l., 16, 15 l. 4°. **†NCOF**

Prompter's manuscript copy.

Smith, Charles. Abbé de l'Epée; or, The orphan; an historical drama, in four acts, translated from the German of Kotzebue [by Charles Smith]. New-York: printed for Charles Smith, 1801. 42 p. 12°. **Reserve**

—— False shame; a comedy, in four acts, translated from the German of Kotzebue [by Charles Smith]. Newark: printed by John Wallis, for Charles Smith, 1801. 63 p. 12°. **Reserve**

—— Fraternal discord; a comedy, in five acts. Translated from the German of Kotzebue [by Charles Smith]. New-York: printed for Charles Smith, 1801. 74 p. 12°. **Reserve**

—— Pizarro; or, The Spaniards in Peru. A tragedy in five acts. Translated from the German of Kotzebue [by Charles Smith]. New-York: printed for Charles Smith, and Stephen Stephens, 1800. 1 p.l., 62 p. 8°. **Reserve**

—— Self immolation: or, The sacrifice of love. A play in three acts. Translated from the German of Kotzebue [by Charles Smith]. New-York: Printed for Charles Smith and S. Stephens, 1800. 54 p. 8°. **Reserve**

—— The wild youth: a comedy for digestion in three acts. Translated from the German of Kotzebue, by Charles Smith. New-York: printed for Charles Smith and S. Stephens, 1800. 74 [really 78] p. 8°. **Reserve**

—— The writing desk; or, Youth in danger. A play in four acts. From the German of Kotzebue. [Translated by Charles Smith.] New-York: printed for Charles Smith, 1801. 72 p. 12°. **Reserve**

Title-page lacking.

Smith, Elizabeth Oakes Prince. Old New York; or, Democracy in 1689. A tragedy, in five acts. New York: Stringer & Townsend, 1853. 65 p. 12°.
NBL p.v.14, no.8

Smith, George Totten. A mistaken Miss. A vaudeville sketch. Chicago: T. S. Denison [cop. 1908]. 11 p. 12°. (Denison's vaudeville sketches.) **NBL p.v.8, no.11**

—— The time table. A vaudeville sketch. Chicago: T. S. Denison [cop. 1908]. 11 p. 12°. (Denison's vaudeville sketches.)
NBL p.v.8, no.18

Smith, S. Decatur, the younger. A man's honor. A drama in one act. Philadelphia: The Penn Pub. Co., 1907. 12 p. 12°.
NBL p.v.8, no.7

—— The Restville auction sale. A farce in one act. Philadelphia: The Penn Pub. Co., 1907. 16 p. 12°. **NBL p.v.8, no.6**

Smith, William Hawley. The new Hamlet, intermixed and interwoven with a revised version of Romeo and Juliet, the combination being modernized, re-written and wrought out on new-discovered lines, as indicated under the light of the higher criticism, by Wm. Hawley Smith and the Smith family, farmers. Printed from the original manuscript, with text in full, and as first produced when done in action by the Smiths, their own company, under the haw tree, on their farm, at the thicket. Chicago: Rand, McNally & Co. ₁cop. 1902.₁ 62 p., 1 port. ob. 16°. **NBM**

Smith, William Henry. The drunkard; or, The fallen saved. A...drama in five acts. New York: S. French ₁18—?₁. 1 p.l., v-vi, 7–64 p. 12°. (French's standard drama. no. 86.) **NCOF**
Prompter's copy, interleaved. With ms. notes.

—— The drunkard. A moral domestic drama of American life, in four acts, by W. H. Smith and a gentleman, adapted to the British stage by T. H. Lacy. London: T. H. Lacy ₁18—?₁. 38 p. 12°. (Lacy's acting edition of plays. v. 7.) **NCO**

Snider, D. J. Clarence, a drama in three acts. St. Louis: E. F. Hobart & Co., 1872. 1 p.l., 45 p. 8°. **NBL p.v.24, no.5**

Sobel, Bernard. Three plays. Boston: Poet Lore Co. ₁1913.₁ 79 p. 12°. **NBM**
Jennie knows. Mrs. Bompton's dinner party. There's always a reason.

Sothern, Edward Hugh. I love! thou lovest! he loves. A monologue. (Metropolitan magazine. New York, 1904. 8°. v. 21, p. 475–481.) ***DA**

Soule, Charles C. A new travesty on Romeo and Juliet. ₁Copyright by Chas. C. Soule₁ as presented before the University Club of St. Louis, January 16, 1877. 50 p. 8°. ***NCS**

Spencer, Edward. Maternus. A tragedy in five acts. Baltimore: J. F. Weishampel, Jr., 1876. 89 p. 12°. **NBL p.v.21, no.9**

Spiller, Burton L. Rock Ford: a drama in four acts. New York: Dick & Fitzgerald, 1909. 54 p. 12°. **NBL p.v.7**

The **Spinsters'** convention. (The original "Old maids' convention.") An evening's entertainment in one scene. Chicago: The Dramatic Publishing Company, cop. 1900. 32 p. 12°. **NBL p.v.11, no.9**

The **Squabble**; a Pastoral Eclogue. By Agricola. With a curious and well-design'd Frontispiece. Printed ₁from The First Edition₁ By Andrew Steuart, in Second-street Philadelphia. 8 p. 12°. **Reserve**

Stanwood, Louise Rogers. The progress of Mrs. Alexander; a farce comedy in three acts. (New England magazine. Boston, 1911. 8°. v. 43, p. 529–560, 655–663.) ***DA**

Steele, Rufus. The fall of Ug; a masque of fear, by Rufus Steele, music by Herman Perlêt. Being the eleventh Grove play of the Bohemian Club of San Francisco, as performed by members of the club, at the thirty-sixth Mid-Summer High Jinks in the Bohemian Grove, Sonoma county. California, on the ninth night of August, 1913. San Francisco: J. Howell, 1913. xiii, 50 p., 1 pl. 12°. ***MZ**

Steele, Silas S. The lion of the sea. A nautical drama in 3 acts, written by Silas S. Steele. ₁186–?₁ 3 v. 12°. **NCOF**
Manuscript promptbook.

Steell, Willis. The death of the discoverer. Philadelphia: H. Murray & Co. ₁1892.₁ 4 p.l., 9–89 p. 12°. **NBL p.v.30, no.3**

Stein, J. J. It's great to be crazy. A farce in one act. Philadelphia: The Penn Pub. Co., 1908. 14 p. 12°. **NBL p.v.6, no.8**

Steiner, Olga. Hard of hearing. Comedy in one act... Chicago: The Dramatic Pub. Co., cop. 1899. 18 p. 8°. (Sergel's acting drama. no. 451.) **NBL p.v.7, no.26**

Stephens, Henry P., and E. SOLOMON. Billee Taylor; or, The reward of virtue. New York: W. A. Pond & Co. ₁188–?₁ 22 p. 12°. ***MZ**

Stern, Edwin M. Hick'ry farm. A comedy-drama of New England life... Chicago: The Dramatic Pub. Co., cop. 1891. 28 p. 12°. (American acting drama.) **NBL p.v.17, no.7**

Stevens, Thomas Wood. The book of words of the pageant and masque of Saint Louis. The words of the pageant by T. W. Stevens. The words of the masque by Percy Mackaye. ₁St. Louis, Mo.: Nixon Jones Printing Company,₁ 1914. 103(1) p. 2. ed. 8°. **NBM**

—— A pageant of the Italian renaissance. ₁In verse.₁ Produced at the Art Institute, Chicago...1909 under the auspices of the Antiquarian Society... ₁Chicago: The Society of Antiquarians, 1909.₁ 85 p. 8°. **NBM**

Stevens, Thomas Wood, and K. S. GOODMAN. Caesar's gods; a Byzantine masque. Chicago: Stage Guild ₁cop. 1913₁. 27 p. 8°. **NBL p.v.28, no.3**

—— The daimio's head, & other masques. The daimio's head, Montezuma, Quetzal's bowl. Chicago: The Stage Guild ₁cop. 1912₁. 2 p.l., 3–32, ₁61₁ p. 8°. **NBM**

—— The masque of Montezuma. Chicago: Stage Guild ₁cop. 1912₁. 16 l. 8°. **NBL p.v.28, no.12**

—— The masque of Quetzal's bowl. Written for the second anniversary of the house warming of the Cliff-Dwellers... [Chicago: Stage Guild, 1912?] 16 1. 8°.
NBL p.v.28, no.5

—— Ryland; a comedy. Chicago: Stage Guild [cop. 1912]. 29 p. 8°.
NBL p.v.28, no.11

Stevenson, Augusta. Plays for the home. With illustrations by E. Boyd Smith. Boston and New York: Houghton Mifflin Company, 1913. vi p., 2 1., 181(1) p. 8°. **NBM**

Plays for children.

Stevenson, Edward Irenæus. The revolt of the holidays. A Christmas gambol. (In: Harper's book of little plays [for children]. New York, 1910. 12°. p. 21–51.)
NBL

Stickney, Joseph Trumbull. Prometheus Pyrphoros. (Harvard monthly. Cambridge, Mass., 1901. 8°. v. 31, p. 45–64.)
STG

Stokes, J. The forest of Rosenwald, or, The Travellers benighted; a melo-drama, in two acts. As performed at the New York Theatre. New York: Dramatic Repository, 1821. 33 p. 16°. **NBM p.v.7**

—— —— New York: E. Murden, 1821. 33 p. 24°. **NCO p.v.253, no.9**

Stone, John Augustus. Tancred; or, The siege of Antioch. A drama in three acts. [By J. A. Stone.] Philadelphia: for the proprietor, 1827. 45 p. 16°. **NBM**

Storrs, Lewis A. The tragedy of Saul, first king of Israel. [A drama.] New York: G. W. Dillingham Co. [1904.] 2 p.l., 7–124 p. 12°. **NBM**

Story, William Wetmore. Nero. [A drama in five acts.] Edinburgh and London: William Blackwood and Sons, 1875. viii, 275 p. 16°. **NBM**

"A **Strange** story." A dramatic sketch in two acts. n. p., n. d. 46 f. 8°. **NCOF**
Prompter's manuscript copy.

Strong, Anna Louise. The king's palace. Illustrated by Margaret Josenhans. Oak Park, Ill.: Oak Leaves Company, cop. 1908. 59 p. 12°. **NBM**

Strong, Grace Cooke. The girl and the undergraduate; a comedy in one act. Philadelphia: Penn Pub. Co., 1912. 20 p. 12°. **NBL p.v.32, no.7**

Stuart, Charles. A chance at midnight; a dramatic episode in one act. New York: Dick & Fitzgerald, 1912. 11 p. 12°.
NBL p.v.27, no.4

Sutherland, Evelyn Greenleaf. Po' white trash, and other one act dramas. Certain of the plays being written in collaboration with Emma Sheridan-Fry and Percy Wallace Mackaye. New York: Duffield & Co., 1909. 5 p.l.,3–232 p., 1 1. 12°. **NBM**

Po' white trash. In far Bohemia. The end of the way. A comedie royall. A bit of instruction. A song at the castle. Rohan the Silent. At the barricade. Galatea of the toy-shop.

Sutherland, Howard Vigne. The woman who could; a play with a purpose. New York: D. FitzGerald, Inc., 1911. 4 p.l., 191 p. 12°. **NBM**

Swartout, Norman Lee. The arrival of Kitty; a farce in three acts. Boston: W. H. Baker & Co., 1914. 181 p. 12°. **NBM**

—— The toastmaster. A college comedy in three acts. Chicago: The Chicago Pub. Co., cop. 1905. 50 p. 12°. (Sergel's acting drama. no. 574.) NBL p.v.4, no.2

Sweimler, James. A vagabond couple; a vaudeville sketch in one act. New York: Dick & Fitzgerald, 1912. 10 p. 12°.
NBL p.v.27, no.13

Talbot, Charles S. Captain Morgan; or, The conspiracy unveiled. A farce in two acts. Rochester: the author, 1827. 22 p. 16°. **NBM p.v.7**

—— Paddy's trip to America; or, The husband with three wives. A farce, in two acts. New York: printed for the author, 1822. iv p., 1 1., 7–48 p. 24°.
NCO p.v.247, no.1

Tamisier. Par le sang. Drame en trois actes et en vers. (Revue canadienne. Montréal, 1905. 8°. v. 49 [année 41, v. 2], p. 346–366, 455–473, 580–610.) ***DM**

Tan-go-ru-a. An historical drama. In prose. Philadelphia: T. B. Peterson, 1856. 280 p. 12°. **NBM**

Tarkington, Booth, and H. L. Wilson. The man from home. [A drama in four acts.] New York: Harper & Bros., 1908. 7 p.l., 13–175(1) p., 8 pl. 8°. **NBM**

Tassin, Algernon. Rust; a play in four acts. New York: Broadway Pub. Co. [1911.] 172 p. 8°. **NBM**

Taurus-Vertus, pseud. The vendetta. A semi-local tragedy. New-Orleans, 1870. 30 p. 8°. **NBL p.v.10, no.7**

Tayleure, Clifton W. Horseshoe Robinson; or, The battle of King's Mountain. A legendary patriotic drama, in three acts. New York: S. French, cop. 1858. 40 p. 16°. (French's standard drama; acting edition. no. 213.) **NCOF**
Prompter's copy, interleaved. With ms. notes.

Taylor, Bayard. The masque of the gods. Boston: J. R. Osgood, 1872. 48 p. 12°. **NBM**

—— The prophet: a tragedy. Boston: James R. Osgood and Company, 1874. 3 p.l., 9–300 p. 12°. **NBI**

Taylor, C. W. The drunkard's warning. A temperance drama, in three acts. Chicago: The Dramatic Publishing Company [18—?]. 38 p. 12°. (Sergel's acting drama. no. 260.) **NBL p.v.3, no.9**

—— New York: Happy Hours Co. [18—?] 41 p. new ed. 12°. (The acting drama. no. 54.) **NBL p.v.5, no.12**

Tecumtha, pseud. See **Ropp**, Edwin Oliver.

Tees, Levin C. A rogue's luck; or, A man of nerve. A farce comedy in three acts. New York: Dick & Fitzgerald, 1909. 46 p. 12°. **NBL p.v.7**

Thaumazo, F., pseud. See **Loevius**, Frederick.

Thiele, M. R. The wager of Gerald O'Rourke. Christmas drama in three acts. From a story by Francis J. Finn. Transposed by M. R. Thiele. New York: Benziger Bros., 1902. 47 p. 12°. **NBL p.v.20, no.7**

Thomas, Albert Ellsworth. Her husband's wife; a comedy in three acts. With an introduction by W. P. Eaton. New York: Doubleday, Page & Co., 1914. x, 133(1) p. 12°. (Drama League series of plays. v. 6.) **NBM**

Thomas, Augustus. Alabama; a drama in four acts. Chicago: Dramatic Pub. Co., 1905. 2 p.l., 148 p. 8°. **NBM**

—— Arizona; a drama in four acts. Chicago: Dramatic Pub. Co., 1904. 2 p.l., (1)8–155 p., 12 pl. 8°. **NBM**

—— As a man thinks; a play in four acts. New York: Duffield & Company, 1911. 213 p., 1 port. 8°. **NBM**

—— The witching hour; a play. (In: T. H. Dickinson, Chief contemporary dramatists. Boston, 1915. 8°. p. 317–355.) **NAFH**

Thomas, Edith Matilda. A new year's masque, and other poems. Boston: Houghton, Mifflin and Company, 1885. v, 138 p. 12°. **NBI**

A new year's masque, p. 1–8.

Thomas, Lewis F. Cortez, the conqueror. A tragedy in five acts... Washington: B. W. Ferguson, 1857. viii p., 1 l., 11–73 p. 8°. **NBM**

Thompson, Alice C. Aunt Matilda's birthday party. A play for girls. Chicago: T. S. Denison [cop. 1908]. 19 p. 12°. (Amateur series.) **NBL p.v.8, no.20**

—— Fudge and a burglar. A farce for girls. Chicago: T. S. Denison [1907]. 8 p. 12°. (Amateur series.) **NBL p.v.6, no.15**

—— Her scarlet slippers: a comedy in one act. Philadelphia: The Penn Publishing Co., 1908. 14 p. 12°. **NBL p.v.6, no.10**

—— A suffragette baby; a comedy in one act. Philadelphia: Penn Pub. Co., 1912. 18 p. 12°. **NBL p.v.32, no.8**

—— The wrong baby. A farce... Chicago: T. S. Denison [1907]. 13 p. 12°. (Amateur series.) **NBL p.v.6, no.16**

Tietzelieve, Julius Tietze. Francisco Ferrer; a tragedy in 5 acts [and in verse], by Julius Tietze. New York, N. Y.: N. Y. Dramatological Pub. Co., 1912. 1 p.l., (1) 6–83 p. 12°. **NBM**

—— Goldie Pride; a play in five acts. New York: Ewald Bros., 1906. 3–4 p., 2 l., 75 p. 16°. **NBM**
Imprint of New York Dramatological Co. pasted over original imprint.

—— Robert Emmet, Ireland's patriot martyr. A political tragedy in 5 acts. New York: R. Auerbach, 1902. 78 p. 12°. **NBL p.v.15, no.14**

Tiffany, Esther B. Anita's trial; or, Our girls in camp. A comedy in three acts for female characters only. Boston: W. H. Baker & Co. [cop. 1889.] 42 p. 12°. (Baker's edition of plays.) **NBM (Tiffany), p.v.1**

—— An autograph letter. A comedy in three acts. Boston: W. H. Baker & Co. [cop. 1889.] 42 p. 12°. (Baker's edition of plays.) **NBM (Tiffany), p.v.1**

—— Bachelor maids. A comedy in one act... Boston: W. H. Baker & Co. [cop. 1897.] 12 p. 12°. (Baker's edition of plays.) **NBM (Tiffany), p.v.1**

—— A model lover. A comedy in two acts. Boston: W. H. Baker & Co. [cop. 1889.] 22 p. 12°. (Baker's edition of plays.) **NBM (Tiffany), p.v.1**

—— A tell-tale eyebrow. A comedy in two acts. Boston: W. H. Baker & Co. [cop. 1889.] 23 p. 12°. (Baker's edition of plays.) **NBM (Tiffany), p.v.1**

—— That Patrick! A comedy in one act. Boston: W. H. Baker & Co. [cop. 1889.] 13 p. 12°. (Baker's edition of plays.) **NBM (Tiffany), p.v.1**

—— The way to his pocket. A comedy in one act. Boston: W. H. Baker & Co. [cop. 1889.] 24 p. 12°. (Baker's edition of plays.) **NBM (Tiffany), p.v.1**

—— Young Mr. Pritchard. A comedy in two scenes. Boston: W. H. Baker & Co. [cop. 1889.] 17 p. 12°. (Baker's edition of plays.) **NBM (Tiffany), p.v.1**

Tilden, Len Ellsworth. The stolen will. A comedy drama in three acts. Boston: W. H. Baker & Co. [cop. 1881.] 58 p. 12°. (Baker's edition of plays.) **NBL p.v.15, no.13**

Toler, Sallie F. Bird's island. A drama in four acts. Chicago: The Dramatic Publishing Company [cop. 1897]. 1 p.l., 5–42 p. 12°. (American acting drama.) **NBL p.v.20, no.8**

Tooker, Gertrude Fulton. Everychild. A play in three acts. With illustrations by Archie Gunn. Indianapolis: The Bobbs-Merrill Company ₍cop. 1914₎. 6 p.l., 141(1) p., 7 pl. 12°.   **NBM**

Torrence, Frederic Ridgely. Abelard and Heloise. ₍Drama in four acts.₎ New York: C. Scribner's Sons, 1907. 4 p.l., 215 p. 12°.   **NBM**

—— El Dorado. A tragedy. New York: J. Lane, 1903. 132 p., 1 l. 12°. **NBM**

Townsend, Charles. Broken fetters. An original drama in five acts. Chicago: The Dramatic Publishing Company, cop. 1890. 32 p. author's ed. 12°. (Sergel's acting drama. no. 356.) **NBL p.v.3, no.11**

—— Capt. Racket. A comedy in three acts. Chicago: The Dramatic Publishing Company ₍cop. 1898₎. 40 p. 12°. (Sergel's acting drama. no. 414.)
          NBL p.v.3, no.12

—— Higbee of Harvard. A comedy drama in three acts. Boston: W. H. Baker & Co., 1906. vi, 7–58 p. 12°. (Baker's edition of plays.)   **NBL p.v.5, no.14**

—— The pride of Virginia. An original comedy drama in four acts. Chicago: The Dramatic Publishing Company ₍cop. 1901₎. 38 p. 12°. (American acting drama.)
          NBL p.v.15, no.10

—— Rio Grande. An original drama in three acts. Boston: W. H. Baker & Co. ₍cop. 1891.₎ 44 p. 12°. (Baker's edition of plays.)   **NBL p.v.15, no.2**

—— The spy of Gettysburg. An original drama in four acts. Boston: W. H. Baker & Co. ₍cop. 1891.₎ 38 p. 12°. (Baker's edition of plays.)
          NBL p.v.15, no.11

—— Too much married. A farce in one act. Philadelphia: Penn Pub. Co., 1905. 24 p. 12°.   **NBL p.v.1, no.9**

—— Uncle Rube. An original drama in four acts. Chicago: The Dramatic Publishing Company ₍cop. 1899₎. 56 p. 12°. (Sergel's acting drama. no. 430.)
          NBL p.v.3, no.10

—— The vagabonds. An original drama in three acts. Boston: W. H. Baker & Co. ₍cop. 1895.₎ 31 p. 12°. (Baker's edition of plays.)   **NBL p.v.15, no.15**

Townsend, George Alfred. President Cromwell. A drama in four acts. New York: E. F. Bonaventure ₍cop. 1884₎. 94 p. 8°.   **NBM**

no. 80 of 200 copies printed.

Trask, Kate Nichols. In the vanguard. ₍Drama in three acts.₎ New York: Macmillan Co., 1913. 3 p.l., 3–148 p. 12°.
          NBM

—— King Alfred's jewel. ₍Drama.₎ London: J. Lane, 1909. vii, 180 p., 1 p. l. 12°.
          NBM

The **Traveller** returned. ₍A comedy in five acts.₎ (In: Mrs. J. S. Murray, The gleaner. Boston, 1798. 12°. v. 3. p. 116–163.)   **Reserve**

Travis, John Coleridge, and MARIE HUNTINGTON. The simple life. An American play in four acts. ₍Peekskill, N. Y.: The Highland Democrat Print, 1908.₎ 3 p.l., 107 p. 12°.   **NBM**

Trent, John Jason. Owin' to Maggie. A comedy in one act. Boston: Walter H. Baker & Co., 1904. 28 p. 8°.   **NBM**

Les **Trois** comédies du "Statu quo" 1834; avec une préface par N. E. Dionne. Québec: Laflamme & Proulx, 1909. 2 p.l., (1) 8–246 p. 12°. (Galerie historique. v. 2.)
          HWD (Galerie)

Ascribed to David Roy, G. B. Faribault, and others.

Troubetzkoy, Amélie Rives, princess. Athelwold. ₍Drama in five acts and in verse.₎ New York: Harper & Bros., 1893. 4 p.l., 117(1) p., 8 pl. 16°.   **NBM**

—— Augustine the man... London: J. Lane ₍1906?₎. 5 p.l., 3–83 p., 1 port. 12°.
          NBM

—— Herod and Mariamne. A tragedy. Philadelphia ₍cop. 1888₎. 305–389 p. 8°.
          NBM

Repr.: Lippincott's monthly magazine. Sept., 1888.

Trowbridge, John Townsend. Coupon bonds: a play in four acts. Boston: W. H. Baker & Co. ₍cop. 1889.₎ 39 p. 12°. (Baker's edition of plays.)
          NBL p.v.15, no.12

—— Neighbor Jackwood. A domestic drama in five acts. Boston: Phillips, Sampson & Co., 1857. 72 p. 12°.
          NBL p.v.5, no.13

Trumbull, David. The death of Capt. Nathan Hale. A drama, in five acts. Written for the Hale Monument Association. Hartford: E. Geer, 1845. 32 p. 8°.
          NBL p.v.24, no.4

Tubbs, Arthur Lewis. Too much Galatea. A farce in one act. Philadelphia: Penn Pub. Co., 1904. 19 p. 12°.
          NBL p.v.1, no.10

Tullidge, Edward W. Ben Israel; or, From under the curse. A Jewish play in five acts. Salt Lake City: J. C. Graham, 1875. v, 7–52 p., 1 l. 8°. **ZZMG p.v.20, no.3**

Turnbull, John D. Rudolph; or, The robbers of Calabria; a melo drame, in three acts. Boston: B. True, 1807. 47 p. 16°.
          NBM p.v.7

—— The wood dæmon, or, The clock has struck! A grand, romantic, cabalistic, melo drama, in three acts: interspersed with processions, pageants, and pantomime ... Boston: printed by B. True, 1808. 34 p. 16°.   **NBM p.v.5**

The Library copy is imperfect, lacking p. 7–10.

Tyler, Royall. The contrast: a comedy, with an introduction by T. J. McKee. New York: The Dunlap Society, 1887. 1 p.l., xl, 107 p., 1 pl. 8°. (The Dunlap Society. Publications. no. 1.) **NBL**

This edition was limited to 175 copies. Reprinted from the 1790 edition of Prichard & Hall, Philadelphia.

Ullmann, Margaret. Pocahontas; a pageant. ₁In four acts, and in verse.₁ Boston: Poet Lore Co. ₁1912.₁ 5 p.l., 9–86 p. 12°. **NBM**

Ulrich, Charles. A daughter of the desert. A comedy drama of the Arizona plains, in four acts. Chicago: T. S. Denison ₁cop. 1908₁. 70 p. 12°. (Alta series.) **NBL p.v.8, no.13**

—— The dawn of liberty, a colonial comedy drama in four acts. Chicago: The Dramatic Pub. Co., cop. 1905. 73 p. 12°. (Sergel's acting drama. no. 576.) **NBL p.v.4, no.4**

—— "Nugget," a Western play in four acts. Chicago: The Chicago Pub. Co. ₁cop. 1905.₁ 51 p. 12°. (Sergel's acting drama. no. 575.) **NBL p.v.4, no.1**

—— On the Little Big Horn. A comedy drama of the West in four acts. Chicago: T. S. Denison ₁1907₁. 82 p. 12°. (Denison's acting plays.) **NBL p.v.6, no.18**

Upside down. An original philosophical and mythological comedy, in five acts, with appropriate tableaux. By Peter Sparks, gentleman. New Orleans: Commercial Bulletin Office, 1871. 31 p. 12°. **NBL p.v.1, no.8**

Upson, Arthur. The city: a poem-drama, and other poems. New York: The Macmillan Co., 1905. vi p., 1 l., 134 p. 12°. **NBI**

Van Dyke, Henry. The house of Rimmon. A drama in four acts. New York: C. Scribner's Sons, 1908. 4 p.l., 5–121 p., 1 pl. 12°. ***PSQ**

First published in Scribner's magazine, v. 44, p. 129–147, 283–300.

Van Noppen, Leonard. Who is Bashti Beki? From ₁the advance sheets of₁ "Armageddon." In verse. ₁Lynchburg, Va.: Brown-Morrison Co., 1912.₁ 32 p. 8°. **NBL p.v.26, no.8**

Varley, J. P. Sylvian: a tragedy; and poems. New York: Brentano Bros., 1885. v p., 1 l., 208 p. 12°. **NBI**

Ver Planck, Mrs. J. Campbell. Sealed instructions: an original comedy-drama in four acts... New York, 1885. 60 p. 12°. bd. as 8°. **NCOF**

Prompter's copy, interleaved. With ms. notes.

Vermont, Adolph. Esther Wake; or, The spirit of the regulators. A play in four acts. Raleigh, N. C.: Edwards & Broughton Printing Co., 1913. 74 p. 8°. **NBM**

Viereck, George Sylvester. A game at love, and other plays. New York: Brentano's, 1906. ix(i), 98 p., 1 l. 8°. **NBM**

A game at love. The mood of a moment. From death's own eyes. A question of fidelity. The butterfly: a morality.

—— —— New York: Moffat, Yard and Co., 1912. ix(i), 92 p., 1 l. 12°. **NBM**

Virtue triumphant. ₁A play in five acts.₁ (In: Mrs. J. S. Murray. The gleaner. Boston, 1798. 12°. v. 3, p. 15–87.) **Reserve**

Vogelsang, G. The creator. Drama, in five acts. Baltimore, 1864. 7 p. 12°. **IK p.v.16, no.9**

Vogl, Virginie Douglass Hyde. Echoes and prophecies: dramatic sparks struck from the anvil of the times by the hammer of the spirit. ₁Westwood, Mass.: Ariel Press, cop. 1909.₁ 193 p., 1 port. 12°. **NBM**

Love and lovers. In ye olde colonie. Dives and Lazarus.

Von Schrader, George Morrison. Salammbo; a tragedy in four acts. ₁In verse. Founded on Flaubert's novel of the same name.₁ Boston: Sherman, French & Co., 1914. 4 p.l., 108 p. 12°. **NBM**

Wagstaff, Blanche Shoemaker. Eris; a dramatic allegory. ₁In verse.₁ New York: Moffat, Yard and Co., 1914. 3 p.l., 41 p., 1 port. 12°. **NBM**

Wainwright, Jonathan Howard. Rip Van Winkle: an original American opera in three acts ₁founded on the story of Washington Irving₁. Music by G. F. Bristow... London: T. H. Lacy ₁18—?₁. 46 p. 12°. (Lacy's acting edition of plays. v. 39.) **NCO**

Walcot, Charles M. Hiawatha; or, Ardent spirits and laughing water. A musical extravaganza, in two acts. New York: S. French ₁cop. 1856₁. 32 p. 12°. (The minor drama. no. 109.) **NBM p.v.2**

—— Nothing to nurse. An original farce, in one act. London: T. H. Lacy ₁1857₁. 19 p. 12°. (Lacy's acting edition of plays. v. 33.) **NCO**

Waldauer, August. Fanchon, the cricket. A domestic drama in five acts, from a tale of George Sand... Chicago: The Dramatic Publishing Company ₁18—?₁. 63 p. 12°. (Sergel's acting drama. no. 432.) **NBL p.v.3, no.13**

—— —— New York: S. French, cop. 1860. 48 p. 12°. (French's standard drama, acting edition. no. 334.) **NCOF (Sand)**

Prompter's copy, interleaved. With ms. notes.

Wallace, J. J. Little Ruby; or, Home jewels. A domestic drama, in three acts. New York: The Dramatic Publishing Company ₁cop. 1872₁. 38 p. author's ed. 12°. (De Witt's acting plays. no. 164.) **NBL p.v.15, no.8**

Wallack, James William. Congreve's comedy of Love for love, carefully revised, curtailed, and altered by J. W. Wallack. New York: D. Appleton & Co., 1854. 2 p.l., (1)10–88 p. 12°. **NCOF (Congreve)**

Prompter's copy, interleaved. With ms. notes.

Wallack, Lester. Honour before wealth: or, The romance of a poor young man. A drama, in four acts. Adapted from the French of Octave Feuillet, by Messrs. Pierrepont Edwards and Lester Wallack. London: T. H. Lacy ₍1868?₎. 54 p. 12°. (Lacy's acting edition of plays. v. 80.) **NCO**

—— The romance of a poor young man. A drama adapted from the French of Octave Feuillet, by Messrs. Pierrepont Edwards and Lester Wallack. New York: Samuel French. cop. 1859. 53 p. 12°. (The standard drama; the acting edition. no. 225.) **NCOF (Feuillet)**

The Library has three prompter's copies of this edition, each interleaved, with ms. notes.

—— The veteran; or, France and Algeria. A drama, in 6 tableaux. New York: S. French ₍1859₎. 63 p. 12°. (French's standard drama. no. 220.) **NBL p.v.13, no.2**

The Library also has a prompter's copy, with ms. notes.

Walter, Eugene. The easiest way; an American play concerning a particular phase of New York life. In four acts and four scenes. ₍New York:₎ printed for the author ₍at the Goerck Art Press, 1909₎. xiv p., 2 l., 121(1) p., 3 port. 8°. **NBM**

Ward, Thomas. Flora; or, The gipsy's frolic; a pastoral opera in three acts. Drama and music by Thomas Ward. New York: French & Wheat, prtrs., 1858. x, (1)12–54 p., 1 l. 8°. **NCO p.v.339, no.4**

Warde, Margaret. The Betty Wales girls and Mr. Kidd. Philadelphia: The Penn Publishing Company, 1912. 61 p. 12°. **NBM**

Ware, Thornton M., and G. P. BAKER. The revolving wedge. A football romance in one act. Boston: W. H. Baker & Co. ₍cop. 1896.₎ 31 p. 12°. (Baker's edition of plays.) **NBL p.v.16, no.2**

Warren, Marie Josephine. The twig of thorn; an Irish fairy play in two acts. Boston: W. H. Baker & Co., 1910. 4 p.l., 96 p. 12°. **NBM**

Warren, Mercy. The group, a farce: As lately Acted, and to be Re-acted, to the Wonder of all superior Intelligences; nigh head quarters, at Amboyne. In two acts. ₍By Mercy Warren.₎ Jamaica, Printed; Philadelphia, Re-printed; by James Humphreys, junior, in Front-street, 1775. 16 p. 8°. **Reserve**

—— Poems, dramatic and miscellaneous. Printed at Boston, by I. Thomas and E. T. Andrews, 1790. viii, (1)10–252 p. 12°. **Reserve**

The sack of Rome. A tragedy, in five acts, p. 13–96. The ladies of Castile. A tragedy, in five acts, p. 97–178.

Warren, Nathan Boughton. Hidden treasure; or, The good St. Nicholas. A Twelfth Night play in three acts... ₍By N. B. Warren.₎ ₍Troy, N. Y., 1881.₎ 35(1) p. 8°. **NBL p.v.25, no.8**

Warren, Walter. Columbus the discoverer. A drama ₍in verse₎. Boston: Arena Publishing Co., 1893. vi, 164 p. 8°. **NBM**

Watterston, George. The child of feeling. A comedy, in five acts. George Town: Joseph Milligan, 1809. 1 p.l., 113 p. 16°. **NBM p.v.7**

Webber, Harry A. Man and wife; dramatized from Wilkie Collins' novel by the same name. Clyde, O.: A. D. Ames, 1873. 48 p. 12°. **NCOF**

Prompter's copy, interleaved. With ms. notes.

Weil, Melanie Alice. Driftwood. Selected sketches in prose and verse. Chicago: Laird & Lee ₍1905₎. 128 p., 1 pl. 16°. **NBY**

The house next door: a comedy in two acts, p. 29–85.

Welcker, Adair. A dream of realms beyond us. San Francisco: the author, 1903. 29 f., 8 p. 5. Amer. ed. 8°. **NBL p.v.24, no.9**

—— —— San Francisco, 1903. 1 p.l., 30 f., 8 p. 6. Amer. ed. 8°. **NBL p.v.24, no.10**

—— Flavia. Berkeley, Cal.: the author, cop. 1885. 118 p. 24°. **NBL p.v.20, no.1**

—— Louis XVI. ₍A drama.₎ 46 f. 16°. **NBM**

Typewritten copy.

—— Romer, king of Norway, and other dramas. Sacramento: Press of Lewis & Johnston, 1885. 2 p.l., (1)10–245 p. 24°. **NBM**

Romer, king of Norway. The bitter end. Flavia. A dream of realms beyond us.

Wells, Charles Henry. Me an' Otis. An original drama in four acts. Boston: W. H. Baker & Co. ₍cop. 1897.₎ 35 p. 12°. (Baker's edition of plays.) **NBL p.v.16, no.3**

Wentworth, Marion Craig. The flower shop; a play in three acts. Boston: R. G. Badger, 1912. 117 p. 12°. **NBM**

—— War brides; a play in one act. illus. (Century. New York, 1915. 8°. v. 89, p. 527–544.) ***DA**

The **Wept** of the Wish-ton-Wish. A drama, in two acts, from J. Fenimore Cooper's novel. (Reprinted in: Alfred Bates, editor, The drama. London, 1903. 8°. v. 19, p. 265–298.) **NAF**

Weston, J. M. Lucretia Borgia. A drama in three acts. Adapted from the French of Victor Hugo by J. M. Weston. Boston: W. V. Spencer [18—?]. 60 p. 12°. (Spencer's Boston theatre. new series, no. 35.) **NCOF**

Prompter's copy, interleaved; with ms. notes.

Whiffen, Edwin T. Samson marrying, Samson at Timnah, Samson Hybristes, Samson blinded. Four dramatic poems. Boston: R. G. Badger, 1905. 190 p. 12°. **NBM**

White, Charles. Black-ey'd William. A nautical Ethiopian sketch, in two scenes. New York: The Dramatic Publishing Company, cop. 1874. 6 p. 12°. (De Witt's Ethiopian and comic drama. no. 11.) **NBL p.v.16, no.6**

—— Sam's courtship. An Ethiopian farce in one act. New York: The Dramatic Publishing Company, cop. 1874. 7 p. 12°. (De Witt's Ethiopian and comic drama. no. 15.) **NBL p.v.16, no.5**

—— Streets of New York; or, New York by gaslight. An Ethiopian sketch, in one scene... New York: The Dramatic Publishing Company, cop. 1874. 6 p. 12°. (De Witt's Ethiopian and comic drama. no. 13.) **NBL p.v.16, no.7**

White, Hervey. The assassin. A tragedy in four acts. Woodstock, N. Y.: Maverick Press [cop. 1911]. 1 p.l., 5–55 p. 8°. **NBL p.v.28, no.7**

White, James Platt. The emancipated; a play. (Harvard monthly. Cambridge, Mass., 1901. 8°. v. 32, p. 184–204.) **STG**

White, John Blake. The forgers: a dramatic poem. Performed at the Charleston Theatre, 1825 and 1826. Reprinted from the Southern literary journal of March, 1837, by order of his son, O. A. White. [New York?] 1899. 59 p. 12°. **NBL p.v.20, no.3**

—— Foscari; or, The Venetian exile. A tragedy in five acts. Charleston: the author, 1806. 52 p. 12°. **NBM p.v.6**

—— The mysteries of the castle; or, The victim of revenge. A drama, in five acts. Charleston: the author, 1807. 68 p., 1 l. 12°. **NBM p.v.6**

White, Lucy. The bird child; a one-act play. (International. New York, 1914. f°. v. 8, p. 337–339.) ***DA**

Wilde, Percival. Dawn, with, The noble lord, The traitor, A house of cards, Playing with fire, The finger of God; one-act plays of life to-day. New York: H. Holt & Co., 1915. 5 p.l., 3–168 p. 12°. **NBM**

—— A question of morality. A comedy in one act. (Century magazine. New York, 1915. 8°. v. 90, p. 609–617.) ***DA**

Wiley, Sara King. The coming of Philibert. New York: Macmillan Co., 1907. 4 p.l., 163 p. 12°. **NBM**

—— Poems lyrical and dramatic, to which is added Cromwell: an historical play. London: Chapman & Hall, Ltd., 1900. 214 p. 12°. **NBI (Drummond)**

Cromwell: an historical play, in five acts, p. 97–214.

Wilkins, Edward G. P. Young New York. A comedy, in three acts. New York: J. Perry [1856?]. 36 p. 12°. **NBM p.v.1**

Wilkinson, Florence. Two plays of Israel, David of Bethlehem, Mary Magdalen. New York: McClure, Phillips & Co., 1904. 2 p.l., 333 p. 12°. ***PSQ**

Willard, Edward. Julius Caesar; an historical tragedy in five acts. [In verse.] Philadelphia: H. Willard [cop. 1890]. 116 p. 8°. **NBM**

Williams, Espy W. H. Parrhasius; or, Thriftless ambition. A dramatic poem. New Orleans: Southern Pub. Co., 1879. 26 p. 16°. **NBI p.v.5, no.7**

Williams, Francis Howard. The higher education. A comedy in two acts. Philadelphia: The Penn Pub. Co., 1907. 43 p. 12°. **NBL p.v.8, no.5**

—— The Princess Elizabeth. A lyric drama. Philadelphia: Claxton, Remsen, & Haffelfinger, 1880. 212 p. 12°. **NBM**

Williams, Henry Llewellyn. L'article 47; or, Breaking the ban. A drama, in three acts, by Adolphe Belot. Translated and adapted to the English stage by Henry L. Williams. New York: R. M. De Witt, cop. 1872. 42 p. 12°. (De Witt's acting plays. no. 137.) **NBL p.v.11, no.8**

—— Isabella Orsini. A romantic drama, in four acts. By S. H. Mosenthal. Translated and adapted to the English stage by H. L. Williams. New York: R. M. De Witt [1870]. 51 p. 12°. (De Witt's acting plays. no. 122.) **NGB p.v.91, no.6**

—— The Lime-Kiln Club in an uproar! An Ethiopian drollery, in one scene. Chicago: The Dramatic Publishing Company, cop. 1891. 8 p. 12°. (The darkey & comic drama.) **NBL p.v.16, no.9**

—— "Marjorie Daw." A domestic comedietta, in two acts. By Miss M. E. Braddon. Prepared for the American stage by H. L. Williams. New York: The Dramatic Pub. Co., cop. 1885. 13 p. 12°. (De Witt's acting plays. no. 338.) **NCO p.v.321, no.12**

Williams, Jesse Lynch. "And so they were married"; a comedy of the new woman. [In three acts.] New York: C. Scribner's Sons, 1914. 5 p.l., 242 p. 8°. **NBM**

Willis, Nathaniel Parker. Bianca Visconti; or, The heart overtasked. [A play in five acts.] New York: S. Colman, 1839.

3 p.l., (1)10–108 p. 12°. (American dramatic library.)   **NBL**

    Bound with: Rufus Dawes, Athenia of Damascus. New York, 1839. 12°.

    The Library also has a prompter's copy of this edition, with ms. notes.

—— Tortesa, the usurer. A play [in five acts]. New York: S. Colman, 1839. 149 p. 12°. (Colman's dramatic library.)   **NBM p.v.1**

    The Library also has a prompter's copy of this edition, with ms. notes.

Willner, W. The book of Esther; dramatized by Rev. W. Willner. Cincinnati: American Hebrew Pub. House, 1892. 32 p. 8°.   ***PSQ**

Wills, Anthony E. Among the Berkshires; or, New England folks. A rural drama in three acts. New York: Dick & Fitzgerald [1906]. 42 p. 12°.   **NBL p.v.1, no.12**

—— College chums. A three-act comedy of college life. New York: Dick & Fitzgerald, 1907. 48 p. 12°.   **NBL p.v.7, no.23**

—— A count of no account. A farce comedy in three acts. New York: Dick & Fitzgerald, 1905. 60 p. 12°.   **NBL p.v.1, no.13**

—— The east siders. A comedy drama of New York life in three acts. New York: Dick & Fitzgerald, 1909. 52 p. 12°.   **NBL p.v.7**

—— The stubborn motor car. A comedy drama in three acts. New York: Dick & Fitzgerald, 1909. 56 p. 12°. **NBL p.v.7**

Wilson, Louise Latham. All on account of an actor. A farce in one act. Philadelphia: Penn Pub. Co., 1904. 15 p. 12°.   **NBL p.v.1, no.14**

—— The fortunes of war. A farce in one act. Philadelphia: Penn Pub Co., 1904. 16 p. 12°.   **NBL p.v.1, no.11**

—— A parliament of servants. A comedy in one act. Chicago: The Dramatic Pub. Co. [cop. 1901.] 20 p. 12°. (Sergel's acting drama. no. 474.)   **NBL p.v.4, no.17**

—— A suit of livery. A farce comedy in two acts. Boston: W. H. Baker & Co., 1902. 24 p. 12°. (Baker's edition of plays.)   **NBL p.v.16, no.4**

Winstanley, W. The hypocrite unmask'd: a comedy in five acts. New York: the author, 1801. 94 p., 1 l. 8°.   **NBM**

Wolter, Herbert. Der grobe Wirt. Schwank in einem Akte. Leipzig: O. Teich [1912]. 23 p. 12°. (Herren-Bühne. Nr. 1.)   **NBL p.v.28, no.4**

Woman against woman; drama in five acts, from the novel of the same name by Florence Marryat. Maud Muller; drama in four acts, from the poem by J. G. Whittier. n. p. [186–?] 96, 43 p. f°.   **NBM**

    Manuscript.

Woodbury, Alice Gale. The match-box. An original comedy, in two acts. Chicago: The Dramatic Pub. Co., cop. 1894. 15 p. 12°. (Sergel's acting drama. no. 400.)   **NBL p.v.4, no.5**

Woodward, T. Trask. The veteran of 1812; or, Kesiah and the scout. A romantic military drama, in five acts. New York: The Dramatic Publishing Company, cop. 1883. 32 p. 12°. (De Witt's acting plays. no. 317.)   **NBL p.v.16, no.8**

Woodworth, Samuel. The deed of gift. A comic opera, in three acts. New York: C. N. Baldwin, 1822. 72 p. 16°. **NBM p.v.5**

—— The poetical works of Samuel Woodworth. Edited by his son. New York: Charles Scribner, 1861. 2 v. 24°.   **NBHD**

    The ninth anniversary of the New York Mirror, July, 1831. A dramatic medley, in one act. v. 2, p. 193–216.

    Shooting stars: or, The battle of the comets. An unwritten tragedy, in two acts. v. 2, p. 217–249.

Woolf, Benjamin Edward. The doctor of Alcantara. Comic opera, in two acts. Libretto by B. E. Woolf. Music by Julius Eichberg. Boston: Oliver Ditson & Co. [cop. 1879.] 30 p. 12°. **NCO p.v.337, no.14**

Woolson, Constance Fenimore. Two women: 1862. A poem [in dramatic form]. New York: D. Appleton and Company, 1877. 92 p. 12°.   **NBI**

Wright, Frances. See **Darusmont**, Frances Wright.

Xerxes the Great; or, The battle of Thermopyle: a patriotic drama. In five acts. Philadelphia: G. Palmer, 1815. 42 p. 16°.   **NBM p.v.9**

Young, Stark. Guenevere: a play in five acts. New York: The Grafton Press, 1906. 82 p. 12°.   **NBM**

Zametkin, Michael. A Russian Shylock; a play in four acts. New York, 1906. 135 (1) p. 12°.   ***PSQ**

Zietz, Edward Shrubb. The reformers; a drama of modern life. In three acts. New York: The Bookery [1912]. 94 p. 12°.   **NBM**

INDEX OF TITLES

Bible plays for the Sabbath school, Leah Levy, 29.
The bicyclers, J. K. Bangs, 5.
The Bigelows' butler, H. O. Osgood, 37.
Billee Taylor, H. P. Stephens and E. Solomon, 45.
Billy Bing, the bachelor from Birmingham, J. M Lévêque, 29.
Billy's chorus girl, Clara B. Batchelder, 5.
The bird child, Lucy White, 51.
Bird's island, Sallie F. Toler, 47.
The birth and death of the prince, L. J. Block, 6.
The birth of Galahad, Richard Hovey, 23.
The birthright, G. B. Hotchkiss, 23.
A bit o' blarney, Fitzgerald Murphy, 35.
A bit of instruction, Evelyn G. Sutherland, 46.
The bitter end, Adair Welcker, 50.
Black-ey'd William, Charles White, 51.
The black tie, George Middleton, 33.
Blanche of Brandywine, J. G. Burnett, 10.
The blockheads; or, Fortunate contractor, 7.
The blood of the fathers, G. F. Lydston, 30.
Bloomer girls, J. A. Fraser, 19.
The blue and the grey, Edward Harrigan, 22.
The blue sphere, Theodore Dreiser, 15.
The Bohemians, E. J. Cowley, 12.
Un bonheur en attire un autre, F. G. Marchand, 32.
The book of Esther, W. Willner, 52.
The book of words of the pageant and masque of Saint Louis, T. W. Stevens, 45.
The Booster Club of Blackville, H. L. Newton, 36.
The Boston dip, G. M. Baker, 4.
Bothwell, J. W. De Peyster, 14.
Bound, Hugh Mann, 31.
Bound by an oath, David Hill, 23.
A box of monkeys, Grace L. Furniss, 20.
The boy Will, R. E. Rogers, 41.
Brangonar, G. H. Calvert, 10.
Brass buttons, Grace A. Luce, 30.
The bread of idleness, E. L. Masters, 32.
Bread on the waters, G. M. Baker, 4.
Breezy Point, Belle M. Locke, 29.
The bride of Fort Edward, Delia Bacon, 4.
Bride roses, W. D. Howells, 24.
Brigham Young, H. J. McKinley, 31.
The bright and dark sides of girl-life in India, Ida O. Phillips, 39.
Broken fetters, Charles Townsend, 48.
Broken promises, S. N. Cook, 12.
Brutus, J. H. Payne, 38.
The Bucktails, J. K. Paulding, 38.
The Buddha, Paul Carus, 10.
Buddha, K. S. Hartmann, 22.
A bundle of matches, Helen P. Kane, 27.
Bunker-Hill, J. D. Burk, 9.
The Buntling ball, Edgar Fawcett, 18.
The burglar alarm, Helen S. Griffith, 21.
Butchers of Ghent, C. H. Saunders, 43.
The butterfly, Lucine Finch, 18.
The butterfly, G. S. Viereck, 49.
By the dead waters, Amelia J. Burr, 10.
Byrd and Hurd, Harold Sander, 42.
Cabestaing, M. J. Cawein, 11.
Cæsar, Henry Peterson, 39.
Caesar's gods, T. W. Stevens and K. S. Goodman, 45.
Caesar's wife, H. B. Hinckley, 23.
Cagliostro, Edward Doyle, 15.
Cain, G. C. Lodge, 29.
Caius Gracchus, Louisa S. C. McCord, 30.
Caius Marius, W. G. Simms, 44.
The cake walk, Frank Dumont, 15.
Calaynos, G. H. Boker, 7.
Caleb, the degenerate, J. S. Cotter, 12.
A call to arms, H. L. Newton, 36.
Calmstorm, the reformer, Cornelius Mathews, 32.
Calvary, Laughton Osborn, 37.
Camille, Matilda Heron, 22.
The candid critic, Epes Sargent, 42.
Candle flame, Katharine Howard, 24.

Canonicus, Alexander Hamilton, 21
The Canterbury pilgrims, Percy Mackaye, 31.
Capriccios, L. J. Block, 6.
The captain of the gate, Beulah M. Dix, 14.
Captain Jack, B. F. Moore, 34.
Captain Jinks of the horse marines, Clyde Fitch, 18.
Captain Kyd, J. S. Jones, 26.
Captain Morgan, C. S. Talbot, 46.
Capt. Racket, Charles Townsend, 48.
Carlotta, Olive T. Dargan, 14.
Carlotta, Robert Roskoten, 42.
The carpenter of Rouen, J. S. Jones, 26.
Carthage, F. S. Saltus, 42.
Cast upon the world, C. E. Newton, 35.
The cat and the cherub, C. B. Fernald, 18.
The cat-boat, Percy Mackaye, 31.
Catharine Brown, the converted Cherokee, 11.
Cecil the seer, G. L. Raymond, 40.
A chafing-dish party, J. K. Bangs, 5.
The champion of her sex, G. M. Baker, 4.
Champlain, J. M. Harper, 22.
A chance at midnight, Charles Stuart, 46.
The chancellor of Egypt, W. T. Beale, 6.
The chaplet of Pan, Wallace Rice and T. W. Stevens, 41.
Charicles, J. P. Quincy, 40.
Charles the Second, J. H. Payne, 38.
Charles di Tocca, C. Y. Rice, 41.
The cheat of pity, George Middleton, 33.
A cheerful liar, J. A. Fraser, 19.
Chihuahua, C. G. Miller, 33.
The child of feeling, George Watterston, 50.
The child in the house, H. H. Howard, 24.
Children of earth, Alice Brown, 9.
A Chinese dummy, Marian D. Campbell, 10.
Christ, K. S. Hartmann, 22.
A Christmas eve with Charles Dickens, Maude M. Frank, 19.
Christmas eve in the South, Dan Collyer, 11.
A Christmas party, Marguerite Merington, 32.
Christus, H. W. Longfellow, 30.
Chuck, Percy Mackaye, 31.
The Church's triumph, M. S. Pine, pseud., 40.
The Cid of Seville, Laughton Osborn, 37.
Cinderella, 11.
Cinderella, Henrietta D. Field and R. M. Field, 18.
Cinderella, C. W. Hubner, 25.
Circles, George Middleton, 33.
The city, Arthur Upson, 49.
Clarence, D. J. Snider, 45.
Clari, J. H. Payne, 38.
Claribel, Walter Malone, 31.
The clerks of Kittery, A. W. Sanborn, 42.
The climbers, Clyde Fitch, 18.
Clio and Lycaon, Nelson Gardner, 20.
A close call, Grace L. Irwin, 25.
The cloud of witnesses, 37.
Clouds, W. A. Silver, 44.
The club friend, Sydney Rosenfeld, 42.
The colleen bawn, Dion Boucicault, 7.
College chums, A. E. Wills, 52.
A colony of cranks, Frederick Loevius, 29.
Columbus, Herman Braeunlich, 8.
Columbus, G. L. Raymond, 40.
Columbus, A. D. Rees, 40.
Columbus the discoverer, Walter Warren, 50.
Columbus el filibustero, John Brougham, 8.
Columbus, the great discoverer of America, 11.
The combat with the dragon, Ethel L. Cox, 12.
Comedies, G. H. Calvert, 10.
A comedy of the exile, Isabella H. Fiske, 18.
The comedy of fraud, S. Crowe, 13.
A comedie royall, Evelyn G. Sutherland, 46.
The comet, Edward Doyle, 15.
The coming of Philibert, Sara K. Wiley, 51.
The coming woman, Arriana R. W. Curtis, 13.
Comrades, G. M. Baker, 4.

Reprint Publishing

For People Who Go For Originals.

This book is a facsimile reprint of the original edition. The term refers to the facsimile with an original in size and design exactly matching simulation as photographic or scanned reproduction.

Facsimile editions offer us the chance to join in the library of historical, cultural and scientific history of mankind, and to rediscover.

The books of the facsimile edition may have marks, notations and other marginalia and pages with errors contained in the original volume. These traces of the past refers to the historical journey that has covered the book.

ISBN 978-3-95940-083-1

Made in
Germany

www.reprintpublishing.com